LANGUAGE AND LITERACY SERIES

Dorothy S. Strickland, FOUNDING EDITOR
Celia Genishi and Donna E. Alvermann, SERIES EDITORS

W9-AUZ-086

(continued)

Literacy for a Better World

The Promise of Teaching in Diverse Classrooms

Laura Schneider VanDerPloeg

Foreword by David Schaafsma

Teachers College, Columbia University
New York and London

Published by Teachers College Press, 1234 Amsterdam Avenue, New York, NY 10027

Chapters 5 and 6 of this book were made possible through a Spencer Foundation Fellowship.

Library of Congress Cataloging-in-Publication Data

VanDerPloeg, Laura Schneider.
  Literacy for a better world : the promise of teaching in diverse classrooms / Laura
    Schneider VanDerPloeg ; foreword by David Schaafsma.
      p. cm. — (Language and literacy series)
  Includes bibliographical references and index.
  ISBN 978-0-8077-5351-4 (pbk. : alk. paper) —
  ISBN 978-0-8077-5352-1 (hardcover : alk. paper)
    1. Literacy—Social aspects—United States. 2. Critical pedagogy—United
  States. 3. Social justice—Study and teaching—United States. I. Title.
  LC151.V36 2012
  302.2'244—dc23   2012024179

ISBN 978-0-8077-5351-4 (paperback)
ISBN 978-0-8077-5352-1 (hardcover)

Printed on acid-free paper

Manufactured in the United States of America

19 18 17 16 15 14 13 12   8 7 6 5 4 3 2 1

For Sophie and Ben—and a better world over the rainbow

Contents

Telling it Rough, or The Meaning of Teaching in a Democratic Society

WHEN I WAS ASKED to write this foreword, I recalled the first years I knew the author of this book in the early 90s, back when she was a participant in the Wisconsin Writing Project I directed and a teacher at a middle school not far from Madison. What I recalled almost immediately about Laura was that she was a poet who, in addition to her interests in democratic teaching (teaching units about the Holocaust, among others things), really liked to teach and write poetry. Around the time I began this foreword, I had been writing a poem about the death of a friend's mother, was honing it, and my memories of Laura's interest in poetry and her passionate commitment to democratic teaching quickly came back to me. It is refreshing to think about democracy and poetry and teaching in the same breath during these challenging times—times of Common Core and NCLB and testing, testing, testing.

Thinking about how a poetic vision of the world might inform the work of developing a democracy, I was just this morning reading from Tess Gallagher's book, *A Concert of Tenses: Essays on Poetry*, in particular her essay, "Sing it Rough," about the writing of her poem, "Each Bird Walking," which tells a story a soon-to-be ex-lover shares with the narrator about devotedly caring for his dying mother. Gallagher's essay, in addition to talking about the process of creating the poem, also describes the process of reading this poem to an audience and getting one woman's baffled observation in response to the poem's title: "But there are no birds in your poem." In other words, what might birds have to do with love and grief? Gallagher acknowledges the fact that there are no literal birds in her poem on the way to sharing her purposes for writing poetry and her way of seeing the world—both of which have little to do with what she calls "1-2-3-4 explanations" of how meaning is made. Poetry, literature, and the making of meaning are not so simple that one can easily identify intentions and purposes and meaning. The process is more intuitive, personal, *mysterious*, and pleasurable than logic might demand. Language and intentionality and meaning are ever so much more complicated than whatever answer "c" is on a Scantron test. And as we think about teaching and learning, we realize that the classroom, too, may be better described in and through a poem than a ledger. What does it mean to teach literacy for democracy, with justice for all? What does it look like?

This book you are about to read honestly and rightly says that things are more complicated and variegated and rich than most textbooks attest; the author makes it clear that, if we are to understand acts of teaching and learning, it is so important to get beyond simplistic assumptions, to see how importantly different and rich language and the humans who use language are! Sometimes "telling it rough," or as Emily Dickinson says, "telling it slant," is more important than any other kind of telling. Laura Schneider VanDerPloeg shows us that to really tell the story of great teaching, we have to teach and tell it rough, tell it messy, tell it as we live it—in all its wondrous complexity.

In this book, VanDerPloeg is in a sense attempting to reconcile two different areas/approaches of literacy teaching: one that focuses on social justice teaching, with an attendant focus on issues of relevance and engagement (a view typically associated with the left or progressive wing of the profession); and one that focuses on strategies, models, techniques, and rigor (typically associated with the right wing of the profession). Notions of rigor and justice almost do not meet in texts on the subject of literacy teaching. The divide is usually depicted as between the critical literacy folks on the left and the critical thinking group on the right. The right is typically better at describing what their view looks like in the classroom, with sets of rigorous and demanding lesson plans. The left is better at vision, at principles for practice, but not so good at showing us what it really, honestly, looks like in practice.

This book is important in that it tells us stories about the process of enacting what the author calls *socially just teaching* that teachers can believe—stories that view rigor and messiness as co-existing. The author tells us, "I don't believe in easy endings to teaching stories or in standardizing outcomes into neat numerical conclusions." She respects us as teachers by admitting and telling stories of her and others'"sideways"moments in teaching and learning. She shares with us principles we can use as a kind of foundation for helping our students read and write for their lives, but she also "tells it rough" so that we can believe she has been there and can show us how to improve what we do.

VanDerPloeg doesn't just inspire us with cool perspectives and ideas about social justice teaching, she shows us how it works in real classrooms with stories of practice; she gives us real strategies to go along with her vision. An important contribution she makes is to link rigor to issues of equity. The right looks at classrooms as a place for a kind of educational triage, where you put all your pedagogical efforts into the Honors kids, the AP kids, the Ones Worth Saving . . . But VanDerPloeg says it is not demanding, rigorous, and successful teaching *until* you speak to issues of social justice. She shows us that great teaching must be both demanding and equitable—that you cannot have equity without high expectations.

It has also been somewhat fashionable for those of us on the left to talk about student learning in ways that de-emphasize the role of the (authoritarian) teacher, but VanDerPloeg proudly flips that script and shows us again and again that teachers and great, focused, rigorous teaching to each and every student makes all the difference. So, are you close to despair, as I often am, about the state of education? Read this book and see it as a map back to sanity—a map to literacy through socially just teaching.

—David Schaafsma, University of Illinois at Chicago

Acknowledgments

I would like to acknowledge the many people whose voices contributed to this book. To Sammy, Katherine, and Nayroby, and the rest of my students from I.S. 306 in the Bronx, thank you for teaching me to listen. Your words have kept me company these many years.

For the teachers who have invited me to spend time in the worlds of their classrooms and to learn from them: many thanks for your gifts of time, talk, and openness in working with me. I especially thank Melissa Baxter (a pseudonym) and Alissa Niemi Heikkila for sharing their practice and the rich life of their classrooms.

My husband, Glen, has been my tireless support and late-night editor for many years now. I am grateful for his love, his editorial talents, and his patient care throughout the process of living and writing this book.

Doug Tuckman—colleague, friend, and writing partner—has read and responded to much of this work as it took shape and as I found my voice in it. I am fortunate to have had such a good reader keeping me company along the way.

Dr. Dave Schaafsma believed I could write this book and inspired me throughout our years of working together to make a difference in the lives of kids. His mentorship and teaching have left a lasting impression on my work and words.

The members of my dissertation committee—Drs. Elizabeth Moje, Lesley Rex, Anne Ruggles Gere, and Carla O'Connor—shepherded my research and work through many revisions and pressed me always to do better.

Finally, I am grateful to the Spencer Foundation for their support of my work, which has sustained me on a long journey from the classroom to this book.

Literacy for a Better World

Minding the Gap
Why We Need Socially Just Teaching

Praxis is reflection and action upon the world in order to transform it.

—Paolo Freire, *Pedagogy of the Oppressed*, p. 28

"TEACHING IS A POLITICAL ACT," my friend and colleague Toby Curry used to say. And I heartily agree. What gets taught, how it gets taught, and why it gets taught—these are serious matters with social and economic consequences for students' lives and futures. As disparities in education persist along the lines of race and class (Yun & Moreno, 2006) and more students drop out of high schools (Alliance for Excellent Education, 2009), we need further attention to what, how, and whom we teach, and strategies through which classroom teaching and learning might achieve more socially just ends.

This book considers the means to those ends: How can the art of reflective teaching praxis—the daily work of enacting socially just pedagogy with students—transform schools and classrooms into places where students learn in ways that embody ideals of equity, empowerment, and social justice?

As North (2009) points out, while the term *social justice* has become the latest catchphrase in education, its meaning can remain elusive. I use the term here to refer to the role education can play in dismantling socially constructed conditions that privilege some groups relative to others through inequitable economic, political, and social systems. Many students in our public high schools experience these inequalities firsthand. They come to school hungry, impoverished, and lacking basic needs. They come to school needing nourishment for their minds but often find they are denied access to the teachers and the learning they require when their zip code impacts the funding, resources, and quality of instruction they receive (Boykin & Noguera, 2011). They struggle for the right to well-being in worlds that exclude them on the basis of identities of *difference*—race, ethnicity, socioeconomic status, gender, sexuality, and ability—and if they cannot advocate for their right to learn, many give up.

Students without access to good teaching, whether because they attend districts with few highly qualified teachers, or because of tracking systems that can subtly segregate students by race and class, face an uphill struggle to learn and graduate with the knowledge and skills they need to be successful. Yet a

I

wide body of research suggests that the quality of instruction students receive
may be their best hope for improving their achievement and for restoring
ideals of equity and opportunity for all to the enterprise of public education
(Darling-Hammond & Richardson, 2009;).

This book uses the terms *social justice* and *socially just teaching* to signify
a pedagogy and set of practices that aim to transform the social contexts in
which students learn and to create opportunities for students to critically examine, resist, and reconstruct social structures and conditions that contribute
to injustice (North, 2006; Shor & Freire, 1985). In the world of school, these
structures shape—and are shaped by—the processes of reading, learning, and
social interaction that happen daily in the classroom. The language arts classroom in particular, where students study the art and use of language to create
worlds and ideas, provides an important site for change: *How* students learn
to read, write, and interact shapes the extent to which they learn to use their
literacies for personal and social good. I speak here of *socially just teaching*
rather than *teaching for social justice* to emphasize process over destination. The
work of teaching in ways that make a better world takes place in the classroom, every day, in even our smallest words and actions. This book focuses on
the notion of teaching as *practice*—the work of scholarly teachers who engage
daily in a process of trying to put principles of equity and justice in action and
who see the work as ongoing rather than "arriving." I want to address the rigor
and messiness of this kind of work and its promise.

This book is intended as a political act; it is meant to be a tool for transforming schools and classrooms. It can be used by language arts teachers and
school leaders to assess issues of equity and engagement in classrooms, and
it can provide a focus for the study of classroom practices (and problems of
practice) for socially just teaching. I hope it will inspire—reawaken—new and
needed conversations about the purpose of education and the important social
and political work that takes place every day in classrooms.

Much good work has already been done in the teaching of reading and writing and culturally relevant instruction. So why the emphasis on social justice?
Because I worry that in our efforts to standardize outcomes for students—to
help "all students achieve" as the rhetoric goes—we may at times be standardizing teaching, learning, and learners in ways that overlook the richness, diversity,
and potential that live in real classrooms. I worry that as we struggle to raise test
scores, we may be forgetting the greater ideals and purposes of education: the
possibility for schools to become equalizers of opportunity (Sizer, 1984).

Using the lens of socially just teaching, we not only consider how to make
student outcomes more equitable, but we also think about what it's all for and
what might be possible. Certainly we want students to leave school with the
skills they need to navigate the worlds of college and work. But we can also
teach in ways that help them become caring members of communities, as

well as learners who have the habits of thinking and practice that can enable them to work with others to build a better, more just society. Building schools and classrooms where students actively engage in a culture of thinking, where their thoughts and ideas matter in their lives and in the social world, and where they have access to powerful teaching that enables them to not only achieve but thrive—I believe these goals are paramount in any efforts that aspire to qualities of social justice. This book is for teachers and leaders who fight this good fight every day.

NAVIGATING THE CHALLENGES OF
TEACHING IN REAL CLASSROOMS

It had been a rough day at work. As an 8th-grade teacher at Intermediate School 306 in the Bronx, I felt—again—like giving up. My students were years behind in reading and math and seemed to want to spend more time arguing with me or with each other than they spent on learning. My lesson for the day had gone sideways a few times already, and my patience was wearing thin. Nothing seemed to be working. Not sure what else to do, I decided to try a *talk*. After all, if there was one thing my students did like to do on a regular basis, it was talk. At that particular moment, it was all they seemed to be doing.

"This behavior right here—I'm worried about this," I said. "We're not getting our work done. We need to talk."

I won't say the room went quiet—being quiet was something my students seldom did—but they listened. We had had a challenging year together; as a class of students who had gone through three teachers the previous year, they fully expected me to leave—and I won't say I didn't consider it. They pushed back on everything I tried to do as a teacher, challenging me to be better every day, to rethink everything I had ever done in the classroom—challenging me to not give up on them. When we had "talks," it was like a family meeting. They listened, but they also let me know exactly what they thought and felt, even if I didn't want to hear it. My students were incredibly strong, honest people, and I needed to learn how to teach them.

"When you leave here," I said, "I want you to have the tools to be whoever you want to be. I want you to be able to read well and think well so that you can solve problems in your life and in your community. I want you to do math well so that you can manage your own life and your money—and so people can't take advantage of you. I want you to be ready and able to go to college if you choose to go, or to be able to do whatever you want in life to pursue your dreams. But I also want you to know how to change the world and make it better—starting with this classroom. When I see what's happening in class right now, I'm worried that we're not getting enough learning done. I'm worried that I'm not doing what I need to do to get you ready, and I want to know what you need to help you learn better here. What can we do about this?"

The discussion that followed touched on everything from expectations, to structures, to the qualities of teachers themselves. My students had experienced a great deal of staff turnover in a lower socioeconomic district that had difficulty attracting highly qualified teachers. One student, Ila, summarized her thoughts as follows: "We just need good teachers, period, Ms. Laura." And while I had experienced success as a teacher in rural Wisconsin, I had found that what makes a "good" teacher was vastly more complicated than I had thought when I arrived in New York and my students challenged me every day. After our talk, I decided to work harder to become the teacher my students needed me to be: structured, impassioned, and relentless (for starters). Not to mention patient.

I don't believe in easy endings to teaching stories or in standardizing outcomes into neat numerical conclusions. I won't say that my students all began reading at the college level or that they passed a state test. I will say that we hung in there together, we built a learning community, and my students began to write and read for their lives in ways that mattered. They became better learners, and I became a better teacher. I came to understand that my students saw social injustice in their lives and communities daily, but that they needed help in understanding why injustice existed and how their learning and literacy might help them do something about it.

I believe that every student has the right to great teachers who can help them build a better world. I believe that, in a world where the ideals of democracy and justice thrive, students' education and opportunities in life are not determined by their zip code, their family's income level, or the color of their skin. To make that vision a reality, we need great teachers in every classroom, period.

Many high school kids come to school as my students did at I.S. 306: resistant, disengaged, unsure whether the promise of schooling applies to them. Some come to school willing to "play the game," going through the motions without truly engaging their minds or hearts in ways that reflect rich learning. José, a high school senior, once said to me when asked to write his own thoughts and ideas in his writer's notebook, "Just give me the work on the board so I can copy it and get out of here!" Sadly, for students like José, education has become an obstacle to overcome rather than a path to greater power and purpose in their lives. By the time many students get to high school, they have years of experience in schooling under their belts, and those years have shaped in countless ways the learners and people they have become when they take their seats in language arts class, or algebra, or world history. Often, the machinery of high school grinds forward, as more students fall behind or check out. Recent concerns over the national high school dropout rate reflect trends that are deeply troubling: Approximately 1.3 million students fail to

graduate from high school every year, the promise of their education unful-
filled (Alliance for Excellent Education, 2009).

When we look closely at who is dropping out of high school, we can hear
a clear call for social justice. According to information on high school graduation from the U.S. Department of Education's National Center for Educational
Statistics, more than half of those failing to graduate are from minority groups.
In many states the difference between White and minority graduation rates
is alarming; in several cases there is a gap of as many as 40 or 50 percentage
points. Class clearly matters in student achievement as well: Young people
between the ages of 16 and 24 who come from the lowest quartile of family
income are about 7 times more likely to drop out than are their peers from the
highest quartile (Alliance for Excellent Education, 2009).

In short: We are failing many of our high school students—especially
lower-income students and students of color. Gaps in achievement that often
begin in elementary and middle school persist across the educational spectrum
until their effects bring a premature end to students' educational careers. Our
response to this dispiriting trend has the power to determine the hopes and futures of generations of students. Given these challenges, how can public education realize its promise of equal opportunity, justice, and strength in diversity?

MAKING A CASE FOR SOCIALLY JUST TEACHING

Every student has the right to a good education—one that affords them the
skills and knowledge to live productive, meaningful lives. No Child Left Behind brought renewed attention to low literacy rates and sparked frenetic
efforts to alter educational outcomes through measures such as standardized
testing, the creation of new standards, and organizational strategies such as
school restructuring, all in the name of closing gaps in school achievement for
marginalized students. Yet none of these measures hit the mark in terms of
focusing on the greatest single factor affecting student achievement outcomes:
classroom instruction.

Research conducted by the University of Tennessee Value-Added Research
and Assessment Center (Sanders & Horn, 1998) examined statewide data on
grades 3 through 5 to study the cumulative and residual effects of teachers
on student achievement in multiple subject areas. The results showed that
the single most important factor in student achievement was the teacher. The
study used value-added modeling to measure teacher effectiveness based on
the amount of academic growth that students made over time. Strong teachers
were therefore identified as those whose students made significant academic
progress regardless of their level of academic achievement when they began.
Students who learned from less effective teachers over the course of 3 years
demonstrated difference in achievement of as much as 50 percentile points less

than their counterparts who had strong teachers during that same time period. The research also showed that lower-achieving students in particular benefit- ed from increased teacher effectiveness and that while less effective teachers produced residual effects on students' learning and achievement, these could be strongly mitigated by achievement gains made possible through instruction by skilled teachers. In other words, powerful teaching holds great promise for making equity of educational outcomes possible. All students, when taught well, can learn well.

Pursuing greater equality in students' educational opportunities and out- comes reflects one important facet of educational projects that aspire to social justice (Noguera, 2007). Defining what counts as socially just teaching and learning can encompass notions of equality, equity, and morality. But what do these terms mean in practice? I like this definition, developed by Leona, a 10th-grader, who wrote this reflection on the meaning of social justice:

> Overall, my definition of social justice, I would have to say is more [about] doing what is right based on equity, but with the strong influence of equality. Equality is like cutting a cookie in half evenly and giving each piece to a different person. Equity is like accidentally cutting one end of the cookie a little bit bigger than the other, then deciding whether to give the bigger half to the starving child or the well-fed child. You would have to think more about the action you're performing, and what would be the right decision.

When we consider the "right decisions" educators face in schools every day, socially just teaching and learning encompasses much more than curriculum.

For example, what is social justice for the 10-year-old who comes to school hungry, who cannot feed himself?

What is social justice for the 9th-grader who would rather get kicked out of class than read *To Kill a Mockingbird*—because she cannot read it?

What is social justice for young men of color who come to school angry and disillusioned because they do not see hope for themselves in their future?

What is social justice for White students whose attitudes sustain racialized beliefs and privileges?

We cannot stop at equity in considering what makes education truly just. Even if we achieve equal numbers on test scores, this will never be enough with- out a justice of caring, a justice of giving students what they need to thrive—and what they need to solve the social problems they live with every day.

To be clear: Socially just teaching belongs in every context and every class- room in order for us to build a better world. Socially just teaching is for my White students in suburban Wisconsin, in a town where the legacy of the KKK and notions of White racial privilege haunted our discussions of Holocaust literature and students' perceptions and understanding of other students and communities. It is for my Puerto Rican, Dominican, and African American students in the Bronx, who saw injustice every day, and in whose mighty voices there was hope for a better future. It is for the sons and daughters of Mexican American immigrants in the rural Yakima Valley, whose parents came to be strangers in a strange land, who worked hard for their children to have opportunities to learn, and who hold out the hope that education can be more just and can make us free.

Socially just teaching is for teachers who see their students as agents for social change, whether in the classroom, the hallways of school, or the community at large. It is for teachers who see social injustices, oppression, and ideologies of difference at work in their classrooms and communities and see in the life of the classroom the opportunity to teach for a greater good. It is for all of the teachers I've known who see their students struggle with the constraints of poverty, who try to teach more with less and less, and who know that education can, quite literally, save a kid's life.

Teaching can be socially just when it provides the means for all students to become literate, independent thinkers and learners. It is socially just when it provides students with what they need to thrive as individuals and as members of communities that strive for better ways to live together. To teach well and for socially just objectives requires not only a grasp of content related to issues of social justice but an understanding of pedagogy, the learning process, and of the particular students we teach.

Recently, renowned educators have spoken of literacy as a civil right that should be provided and guaranteed through public education (Greene, 2008; Plaut, 2009). This right to literacy, as outlined by Plaut (2009), is engendered through meaningful engagement with texts and ideas. It encompasses several dimensions of teaching and learning, including students' active engagement in relevant content, comprehensive thinking about the content, and the power to use learning as a means to transform one's world. To take this right seriously means to insist that every child has not merely the right to literacy but the right to the kind of excellent instruction that makes powerful literacy learning possible.

Socially just teaching makes this kind of learning possible; it is a means to this civil right. To that end, the instructional framework for this book draws on several bodies of research and theory to define socially just teaching practice: Studies of effective literacy instruction and adolescent literacy (Allington, 2007; Alvermann, 2002; Beers, Probst, & Rief, 2007; Nystrand, 1997), studies of how people learn (Bransford, Brown, & Cocking, 2000; Cambourne, 1995; Resnick, 1999), and literature on critical and culturally relevant pedagogy (Banks, 2001; Delpit & Dowdy, 2002; Gay, 2002; Ladson-Billings, 2000). A focus on teaching as practice means that we will consider how these theories play out in the interactions among teacher, learners, and content, or the "instructional core" (City, Elmore, Fiarman, & Teitel, 2009). A focus on these theories and bodies of research help us to seek answers to questions like these:

- How can classroom instruction in language arts provide all students with access to powerful—and empowering—literacy learning?
- How do we make learning culturally and critically relevant so that students can have power in their lives and communities?
- How can literacy teaching and learning help students construct positive identities through socially just learning?

This chapter is intended as a framework or lens through which to view the following chapters in this book: It presents the theory that informs the practice and provides a definition of what socially just teaching practice can look like. It is meant as a tool for educational leaders as well as teachers, for the work of creating powerful educational opportunities for all students is the work not of a single teacher, but of communities of educators working to eliminate inequities and create a better world through the power of teaching and learning.

This framework has several purposes. It can serve as a way to build a common vision for instruction among instructional leaders and teachers, and it can provide a means to assess the current state of instruction in classrooms and throughout schools in order to identify areas for ongoing professional growth. In Chapter 1, I will address and define several dimensions of socially just teaching: *stance, relevance, access, identity*, and *agency*. Each dimension is described in order to illustrate what it can look and sound like in the classroom. Later chapters will provide examples of what various aspects of socially just teaching look like in action. I hope this book will provide food for thought, discussion, and action that holds promise for building a better world, one teacher, student, and classroom at a time.

CHAPTER ONE

Constructing a Vision of Socially Just Teaching

WHAT WE SEE WHEN we walk into a classroom depends on what we are looking for. As a consultant, I work with district leaders, principals, and teachers to focus on building capacity for literacy teaching and learning across educational systems. For that purpose, I regularly lead instructional rounds (City et. al., 2009) to visit classrooms. These visits serve as a means for district leaders and teachers to assess strengths and needs for instruction and to set goals for teachers, students, and principals that can facilitate progress toward equitable instruction and student achievement. On more than one occasion, I have visited classrooms with other educators, only to find out later that we had much different interpretations of what we saw. While I was noticing the kinds of talk and thinking that students did during instruction, the principal, for example, might have focused on whether the teacher had posted the purpose for the lesson on the board. Based on the evidence we attended to, we drew different conclusions about what was happening—and the implications for assessment.

Like all teachers, I have had those days where I worked hard to prepare a lesson and teach well, only to find that something didn't work right . . . a certain *je ne sais quoi.* Someone observing what I did may have noticed a purpose statement on the board or the use of instructional charts, but if students were not engaging in the learning, I would have needed a partner for observation who could help me figure out *why*.

A focus on instructional strategies or curriculum alone cannot ensure that socially just teaching and learning occurs. To focus on learning about instructional practice means that we attend to not only what teachers do in a given classroom, but equally important, to what *students* do. Any process of reflecting on instruction should provide grounds for sense making and inquiry into the interactions among teachers, students, and content.

So what characterizes teaching practice in a socially just classroom? While there are many possible lenses through which to view socially just pedagogy (see North, 2009, for example), I have chosen to focus on five: *stance, relevance, access, identity,* and *agency*. I selected these five lenses because I have found, through work with many secondary classrooms, that they offer critical insight into the discourse and interactions among teachers and students in diverse school contexts and that they have significant bearing on the nature of the learning opportunities students receive. It is my hope that this framework can provide a means for reflection and action on not only what we teach but also how we teach it and to whom.

LENSES FOR DEFINING AND STUDYING SOCIALLY JUST TEACHING PRACTICE

The First Lens: Stance

In her study of the characteristics of effective high schools, Valerie Lee (2001) found that responsibility for learning, the shared ethic that educators themselves are responsible for whether or not students learn, was "consistently, positively, and significantly related to achievement gains in all four subjects," regardless of social background (pp. 92–93). Students from lower socioeconomic backgrounds made significant academic gains in schools with high collective responsibility as compared with students in schools with low collective responsibility.

In many schools and classrooms, education is offered through a kind of buffet-style approach that says to students, *We'll put it all out there for you; take it or leave it. If you don't like it or don't do well, that's on you.* Shifting toward a student-centered stance views education as a dynamic process, one in which students' responses to instruction serve to shape what is offered and how it is offered. It says to students, *Your learning matters to us. Help us understand how you learn best and what gets in the way so we can adapt instruction to meet your needs and help you succeed.*

I have worked with Heritage High School in Marysville, Washington, for over 5 years. Heritage serves students from the Tulalip Indian Reservation and aims to foster students' learning about their cultural heritage and history as members of the Tulalip tribal community. For Marina Benally and Ervanna Little Eagle, both Native teachers, this is profoundly important work to sustain the community's culture and well-being. Together, we have worked to develop instruction that is both culturally relevant and addresses the specific educational needs of the students, many of whom can be resistant to schooling and represent a wide range of academic skills. Marina and Ervanna worry about their students' stance toward learning, which has tended to be very passive. "Our students are more comfortable filling out a worksheet than sharing their ideas in discussion," Marina says. "They've had so many years of passive learning that they resist being asked to think." Part of the teachers' work in the classroom, then, has been to help students develop a different stance toward their learning and to acquire skills for more active reading, writing, and thinking. At the same time, Marina and Ervanna have worked to understand when and how students' engagement falters, how culture matters, and what they can do as teachers to meet students' needs. Their continual research and reflection on their role as educators, their interactions with students, and the sociocultural context for teaching and learning exemplifies a socially just instructional stance. From such a stance, teachers continually seek to improve by adapting their instruction to what they are learning about students.

Corcoran and Silander (2009) propose that this kind of "adaptive instruction" offers the best hope for high schools to reform instruction in ways that can meet the needs of all students. They note that various initiatives to address inequities in learning have focused on the use of research-based strategies and approaches, such as the teaching of metacognitive strategies for reading. While the authors emphasize the importance of promoting proven instructional practices, they stress that these practices must be paired with systematic and ongoing efforts to understand who students are, how they are learning, and what they need—and to adapt instruction accordingly.

In short, teaching stance matters, and when we as educators assume responsibility for students' learning and engagement in school, when we teach as though students' lives depend on it (and they do), we can make a powerful difference in their lives and futures. This requires us to take the stance that our students' educational weaknesses create our greatest opportunities for teaching. If we see that students are not independent learners or thinkers, we recognize opportunities to teach them the habits of mind they need to acquire. If we see a lack of curiosity, a tendency to perform rote tasks but to never ask questions, we perceive an opportunity to teach them to become questioners, inquirers, and knowledge-seekers.

In my own teaching life, in contexts as diverse as rural Wisconsin and the Bronx, students at times talked and acted in ways that reinforced social attitudes of prejudice and exclusion; their beliefs about race, class, and opportunity could work to constrain their lives, futures, and interactions with one another. At the same time, I struggled to meet their diverse needs as readers, writers, and learners, knowing that some of my 8th-graders read at a 4th-grade level while others could read well beyond their grade-level peers. At times I felt paralyzed when it came to addressing the social dynamics and learning challenges of my classroom because of my identity as a White teacher or because I just didn't know how to teach in a way that made students feel both honored and challenged. When students expressed ideas that reflected racial bias or the notion that one's racial identity or class would predetermine the kind of future that was possible, it was perplexing at times to know what to say or do, and tempting often to do nothing at all.

Enacting a teaching practice that reflects values of equity, justice, and empowerment requires ongoing reflection. As I consider my own teaching practice and how my stance affects students' learning, I think about the following questions:

- How will my teaching honor and engage students' identities, interests, and the funds of knowledge they bring from their lives and communities?
- How will my teaching help every student to become a better reader, writer, and thinker?
- How will I design opportunities for learning that engage my students in meaningful content—and ensure a safe, respectful, and inclusive learning community?
- How will I respond to issues of social justice (such as prejudice or exclusion) that arise from my students' reading, learning, and interactions?
- How will my teaching help students to develop and use intellectual tools to shape their lives and communities in empowering ways?

The answers to these questions are complex, contingent, and always shaped by the contexts in which we teach. To determine what is socially just in the classroom requires that we listen so we can understand who students are and from what communities they come. It also requires that we take a stance toward teaching as practice, as the daily attempt to inquire and grow our teaching in ways that best serve those students and communities while enacting ideals of socially just pedagogy. Seen this way, teaching practice requires continual "reflection and action on the world" (Freire, 1972, p. 28)—and the world of the classroom—in order to transform it. Socially just teaching is not something we arrive at, but rather something we strive for daily in a disciplined way.

My students in the Bronx, whose backgrounds and experiences were very different than my own, taught me the importance of shifting my stance as a teacher to understand students on their own terms, and to teach from a place of learning with them, rather than a place of teaching to them as the subjects of my instruction. I came to understand that choosing not to speak to issues of social justice that I observed in students' talk, interactions, and environment (such as racial or gender stereotyping or the high dropout rate that threatened my students' educational futures) was as problematic as addressing them directly; to not speak made me complicit in perpetuating conditions that created and sustained injustices, but to engage students in addressing those conditions at times led me into uncharted territory without a clear path or outcome.

In a pedagogy of socially just teaching, then, the teacher is as much the subject as are the students in the meaning-making process. We navigate a stance that capitalizes on our position as "more knowledgeable other" while also enabling us to learn alongside students and coach them toward greater agency and independence in their learning. In a socially just classroom, students explicitly learn how to apply a critical lens to their reading, writing, and study of language, but we hand over control and ownership of the meaning making to students themselves. Students' responses then become another focus of shared study, for we attend to the meanings students are making and the ways in which students' responses resist, reinscribe, or sustain ideas and ways of thinking that have the potential to constrain their identities and opportunities. Rather than reinforcing particular interpretations or views of texts of events, we can give students the means to confront critical ideas and texts and to make sense of those ideas and their implications for social justice.

When my students at I.S. 306, for example, questioned the value of reading and learning to read, I transformed their resistance into inquiry. Together we considered: What is the value of reading? How does reading affect or shape one's everyday life? As we pursued these questions together, we read and discussed the novel *Nightjohn*, by Gary Paulsen, in which a slave secretly teaches other slaves to read as an act of resistance and empowerment. In an attempt to honor students' questions and their resistance to reading, I considered how reading afforded me power in my own life and looked for models of other powerful readers and thinkers who had used their reading to change their lives and the world around them.

When we consider how stance plays out in classroom practice, we think not only about what the teacher does but about students' roles as well. Figure 1.1 describes what classrooms look like when teachers' and students' stances create a socially just classroom culture.

The Second Lens: Relevance

Opportunities to read and write for relevant, real-world purposes can have a significant impact on students' educational attainment. Studies have shown that engagement with reading critically affects achievement and can even mediate the constraints of socioeconomic status (Cummins, 2007). Arguing against pedagogies that advocate prescriptive, skills-based instruction (particularly in classrooms serving underserved and lower-income students), Cummins cites research by Guthrie (2004), which found that students

> whose family background was characterized by low income and low education, but who were highly engaged readers, substantially outscored students who came from backgrounds with higher education and higher income, but who themselves were less engaged readers. Based on a massive sample, this finding suggests the stunning conclusion that engaged reading can overcome traditional barriers to reading achievement, including gender, parental education, and income. (Cummins, 2007, p. 5)

Figure 1.1. Observing Stance in the Socially Just Classroom

What Teachers Say and Do	What Students Say and Do
Act as co-learner with students, but leverage expertise to benefit students' growth	Act as agents for their own learning in the classroom
View students' lives and experiences as part of the content of the classroom	Pose questions and engage in inquiry work related to social justice in their own lives and communities
Partner with students, their families, and their communities in developing relevant curriculum and instruction	Treat one another as equals and as resources for learning
Model reflective thinking and practice	Practice open-mindedness by entertaining diverse ideas through texts and classroom conversation
Reflect on and assess the nature of the classroom community and the power relationships and meanings at play	Take responsibility for their own learning, as well as the learning and well-being of the group
Model, coach, and lead students in enacting socially just relationships and habits of thinking	
Take responsibility for every learner, making sure students have what they need to be successful	

In a socially just classroom, teachers can make students' literate engagement a priority and focus for instruction by seeking to make learning relevant (Alvermann, 2002; Hammerberg, 2004). Students have opportunities to make choices about their learning and to voice their ideas in ways that help them make meaningful connections to their own lives. Making learning relevant to students goes beyond merely connecting the content of their learning to their lived experience; it also requires attention to the conditions under which they learn. Students need opportunities to determine for themselves what is relevant and how it is relevant. After all, if students only learn content chosen by the teacher and deemed to reflect their lives in literal ways, we risk underexposing them to the rich world of texts, ideas, and possibilities outside their own lived experience.

When I taught 8th-grade language arts in the Bronx, I struggled to find texts and reading experiences that would engage my students. Many of these young people were highly resistant readers. In an effort to help them connect with their experiences of growing up in the city, I chose *The House on Mango Street*, by Sandra Cisneros (1991), as a text to read together. The story, told in a series of vignettes, focuses on the experiences of Esperanza, a Mexican American girl growing up in a poor neighborhood of Chicago. The text uses some Spanish language and draws on Esperanza's rich cultural heritage as a Chicana. It tells stories of discrimination, poverty, and growing up that I thought my students might relate to. However, they hated the text and complained continually about Esperanza's character; they considered her to be a whiny complainer. The text, and my use of it, did not get us far in terms of engagement or in exploring notions of social justice.

Later in the year, I chose another novel, *Lord of the Flies*, by William Golding, because it dealt with issues of power, violence, and community—ideas I wanted my students to consider as part of our life together in the classroom. This book they loved. Students were engrossed in the struggle for power and respect that the characters faced in trying to survive as a community of children stranded on an island. Our discussions caused a turning point in our life together in the classroom—and helped my students experience reading as engagement with powerful, life-changing ideas.

Choosing what makes learning relevant for students is an act of power. After all, who determines what is relevant for whom? How we choose the texts and ideas that students will work with in the classroom can serve to position them as subjects or as agents. While intending to provide relevant instruction for my students through our reading of *The House on Mango Street*, I found instead that students resisted the text and how they felt it positioned urban people of color. In considering the work of socially just teaching, it is therefore important to consider how students' purpose for learning is framed and what role students will play in determining that purpose. While *Lord of the Flies* focuses on the experiences of White British boys during World War II and may not be a traditional choice for multicultural literature in a socially just pedagogy, the text helped our classroom community explore issues that were deeply purposeful and relevant to their life inside and outside of class. Many of my students had experienced violence in the community and struggled for respect and power with one another in the classroom; Golding's text therefore provided an opportunity for critical reflection on their experiences and relationships. Because of the book, our relationships with one another changed.

My point is not to argue against the inclusion of more diverse, multicultural texts in the classroom. On the contrary, the use of texts representing multiple perspectives and cultural backgrounds is critical for building a learning context for inclusion and social justice work. The problem comes with the choosing— and the extent to which students can name and inform what is relevant for themselves. While conducting research in Detroit schools, I met Tyrone, an African American high school student who shared his frustrations with the district curriculum. "All we ever learn about is Black history," he complained. "I've been learning about that since elementary school and I'm tired of it." While the district curriculum was intended to be relevant for Tyrone as an African American, his response reflects, ironically, the problem of student disengagement with content deemed by others to be relevant for the learner. This dilemma poses further challenges for enacting socially just teaching in ways that honor what the learner deems relevant for him- or herself, while also pressing the student to consider how new learning might be relevant in previously unimagined ways.

The notion of relevance involves more than considerations of culture, however. Creating powerful educational opportunities should also be relevant to the authentic work of the disciplines under study. Students need to be steeped in learning the habits of thinking that characterize the disciplines (Schoenbach, Greenleaf, Cziko, & Hurwitz, 1993; Ritchhart, 2002) and in learning to think critically with texts and ideas specific to those disciplines. While a pedagogy of socially just teaching focuses and builds on the ideas of students, it should also help them understand and position themselves as part of a larger community of thinkers. It is not enough for students to learn about historical situations of social injustice if they do not also develop the skills for reading, writing, and thinking as historians. It is not enough to read about social injustice in a novel like *Beloved*, by Toni Morrison, without also learning the habits of mind of literary scholars and sophisticated readers. Content without process (and vice versa) cannot sufficiently empower students to think and act for social good with the intelligence and grace required. Figure 1.2 describes what the quality of relevance looks like in classrooms characterized by socially just teaching and learning.

The Third Lens: Access

All students have the right to learn to read, write, and think well; every teacher can help them get there. It is not enough to engage students in

Figure 1.2. Seeing Relevance in the Socially Just Classroom

What Teachers Say and Do	What Students Say and Do
Capitalize on students' interests and the needs of the community by developing responsive curriculum	Express how and why their learning matters for their lives and communities
Create conditions for students to develop purpose for their own learning	Set purposes for their own learning, assess what they need to be successful, and advocate for the support they need
Help students to analyze how power relationships shape the contexts in which language and knowledge are used	Know how the content and skills they are learning will give them access to identities, opportunities, and political resources for navigating social and economic systems
Help students understand how to use their reading, writing, and thinking skills in diverse contexts and situations	
Create learning opportunities that prepare students for college, work, life and social action	Practice using literacy for meaningful audiences and purposes

discussions about issues of social justice and equity if, at the end of the day, they cannot independently gain access to knowledge about those issues through reading, writing, or thinking. To have access to learning in ways that are empowering, students need rich, relevant purposes for reading, writing, and learning—along with the skills to enact those purposes. Socially just teaching facilitates students' access to powerful texts and ideas not only by exposing students to texts that help them develop their thinking but also by helping them learn how to read those texts well.

Several years ago, I worked with a small group of history teachers in a socioculturally diverse high school outside Seattle. The teachers were committed to ideals of social justice and had planned to have students learn about civil disobedience by studying the writings of Mohandas Gandhi. Yet students had difficulty understanding the text and making sense of Gandhi's exquisite arguments for nonviolence. As we worked together in the classroom, I modeled and coached students through an understanding of the text, giving them opportunities to both observe my thinking process with the text and to engage in supported strategy work as they made meaning of the text on their own. Teachers saw students struggling—but succeeding independently—in making sense of Gandhi's writing. Rather than seeing promise, however, they were dismayed. "This takes a long time," they worried. "How will we get through the rest of our curriculum?"

I argue that if students can't independently access the content we're trying to teach them, then "getting through it" won't ultimately serve them well—or accomplish socially just objectives. What good is it to learn about Gandhi as a 10th-grader if you can't read and understand his ideas for yourself? This puts students in the position of becoming passive learners who rely on the interpretations and readings of their teachers rather than helping them become independent readers who can critically engage with texts and ideas on their own.

To create access to learning requires not only that educators make learning relevant but also that we explicitly teach the reading, writing, and thinking work in which we want students to engage. It requires that we scaffold students' learning and that we work daily to co-construct an inclusive and supportive classroom community to facilitate their access to learning.

Figure 1.3 illustrates what we might see in classrooms that provide students with access to empowering learning.

The Fourth Lens: Identity

Socially just teaching practice recognizes, respects, and builds upon the identities, backgrounds, and experiences of students and fosters belonging in a community of learners (Ballenger, 1999; Ladson-Billings, 2000; Moll, 1992). Because identities shape how we perceive and make sense of what we are

Figure 1.3. Seeing Access in the Socially Just Classroom

What Teachers Say and Do	What Students Say and Do
Provide rigorous instruction to actively engage students in high-level intellectual work	Actively read, write, and think to construct meaning
Create an inclusive classroom environment that fosters engagement, collaboration, and interdependence	Demonstrate effort in order to grow as learners
	Take risks in learning and advocate for what they need
Create opportunities for all students to learn the same content, ideas, and skills	Engage in opportunities to learn the same content, ideas, and skills, regardless of academic tracking or socioeconomic background
Assess students' reading, writing, and thinking skills to determine where explicit instruction and coaching are needed	Know how the content and skills they are learning will give them access to identities, opportunities, and political resources for navigating social and economic systems
Use students' funds of knowledge and sociocultural experiences to help students learn and understand	Draw on funds of knowledge and sociocultural experience to create meaning and develop understanding

learning, they influence how we use our learning to engage with the world around us. This is particularly important for adolescent learners, whose social worlds at school provide an important context for their meaning making and shape how they view themselves and others.

In the course of learning, students experience and engage with a variety of what Gee (1999), a literacy researcher, calls Discourses, or "ways of acting, interacting, feeling, believing, valuing together with other people and with various sorts of characteristic objects, symbols, tools, and technologies" (p. 7). When students' talk enacts particular Discourses (based, for example, on ideas of what it means to be a man or woman, or to belong to a particular racial or ethnic group), this serves as a means for students to construct identities that have social value for them: Students often take up Discourses in order to be recognized as a particular sort of person (e.g., "jock")—and they may be positioned by others on the basis of the identities those Discourses afford. In one classroom study, for example, the researcher (Leander, 2002) noted how a student, Latanya, developed a "ghetto" identity in the classroom through her talk and interactions with other students in the class. This identity negatively shaped how she was viewed as a student and how she participated as a learner in the classroom context. As this example illustrates, identity can matter a great deal to students' engagement and meaning making in school.

Identity relies on recognition. We say that someone "has" a certain identity because the person is recognized by others as being "that sort of person." This is not to say that identities are uniform or singular; my own identity is a hybrid built from the different aspects of my life: mother, teacher, White woman, scholar, and Seattleite, to name a few. Similarly, our students may be recognized by their race, ethnicity, socioeconomic status, academic persona (such as class clown or "brain"), or other markers deemed important in the social world of school. Discourses afford students varying social positions with different degrees of power and agency; they are part of the naturalized social order that students enter into and in which they (and we) participate.

In a socially just classroom, teachers strive to create an inclusive classroom culture in which power relations among students are equitable and just, providing a safe space in which diverse ways of thinking and being are welcomed. At the same time, socially just teaching enables students to understand identities as social constructions—ideas about people that are socially created and sustained to serve particular purposes. Helping students understand how identities work enables them to analyze how identities are socially positioned and how this positioning mediates individuals' access to social and political power and resources. It's not enough for students to merely respect diverse identities in a socially just classroom without understanding how ideas about difference and identity can shape people's lives and opportunities.

Teaching in ways that enable students to consider and create healthy, empowered identities requires complex work, to say the least. Yet as Allington (2007) notes, "All teacher talk imputes intentions, positions, and identities as well as communicating curriculum-relevant information" (p. 284). This is true of teachers who aspire to socially just practices—and those who do not. Because students' identities as learners and human beings are built every day through their conversations and interactions with others, and because the work of adolescents is largely the work of "becoming someone" by developing identities in the social world (as reader, writer, human being), the ways in which identity building takes place in classrooms matters immensely.

Consider, for example, the following classroom interaction during a 9th-grade class I observed during their discussion of the play *A Raisin in the Sun*, by Lorraine Hansberry. The play focuses on the experiences of an African American family in Chicago during the 1950s and illustrates how their access to the American Dream was hindered by institutionalized racism. The family tries to buy a home in a predominantly White neighborhood and is prevented from doing so by the White realtor and neighborhood association. During the first scene of Act 1, the main character, Walter, complains that his wife does not understand his dreams as a Black man. As this particular group of 9th-grade students read the scene together, the following interaction occurred:

A student read aloud the dialogue on page 34 in which the character of Walter complains to his wife, "We one group of men tied to a race of women with small minds!" (Hansberry, 1958/1988).

Edward, an African American student, commented, "Why do they have to talk that way?" The teacher (who was White) paused momentarily, and Edward repeated, "Why do they have to talk that way, like we all one [people]?" (Field notes, April 26, 2005)

In this moment, Edward introduced issues of race and identity as part of the group's process of making sense of the text. Although the text reflects important issues pertaining to social justice and race, Edward expressed concern over how the text portrays the identities of African Americans and whether or not this reflects a "we" to whom he belonged. In this small moment of classroom reading and interaction, identity played a powerful part in his engagement with the text.

Lotan (2006) notes that these moments can have critical consequences for perpetuating inequities in the classroom. Edward's response may have signaled that he recognized a kind of *stereotype threat* (Steele, 1997) realized through his reading of the text. Although the fictional character of Walter makes this offhand comment to his wife in the context of Hansberry's work of dramatic art, for Edward and other African American males in a heterogeneous classroom this reading experience held the potential to undermine intellectual identity and performance because of the explicit positioning of racial identity.

While ideas about identity and positioning will be explored in Chapters 5 and 6 through specific examples of instruction, the list captured in Figure 1.4 creates a starting point for describing how identity matters in the practice of socially just teaching.

The Fifth Lens: Agency

When I think about my years of classroom teaching, I am grateful to students who challenged me with the question "Why are we doing this?" Their questions continually helped me to think more deeply, more carefully, about the purposes for our learning work and how I might better help students develop agency in their learning and their lives. High school students in particular have had over 9 years of experience in educational systems and have often begun to question, rightly, the purpose for their learning. This is no small question, particularly in a frantic age of testing and accountability.

I first heard this question put to me as a student teacher at Mabel Dean Bacon Vocational High School in the Lower East Side of Manhattan. My students, who were seniors, had made it through their entire school career

Figure 1.4. Seeing Identity at Work in Socially Just Teaching

What Teachers Say and Do	What Students Say and Do
Create a space for students to enact and discuss social identities (raced, classed, gendered)	Express and make meaning of their identities in the social world
Actively help students to define and construct what it means to be a community member, citizen, advocate, and learner	Draw on and discuss the identities they navigate in their daily lives and how those mediate their understandings
Help students to create positive interactions and conversations in which diverse identities can be discussed and valued	Accept one another as diverse class members sharing a common bond of learning
Give all students access to powerful academic identities by setting high expectations for all students to succeed	Engage in constructing positive, purposeful academic and social identities for themselves through their reading, writing, speaking, and engagement in learning
Choose texts that offer students images of diverse and empowering racial, ethnic, gender, and socioeconomic identities	Read, write, and reflect on how identities "work" as social constructs
Consider how the identities offered in texts might contribute to stereotypes, and choose texts that provide opportunities to construct healthy, empowered identities	Understand how identities can influence access to opportunities and resources
Consider how the texts used in the classroom may position students' identities and work with texts in ways that create a safe space for inquiry	

without doing much of what I asked of them: to write their own thoughts and ideas. On one memorable day, several students stood up and angrily demanded to know, "Why do we have to do all this writing? Can't you just put the notes on the board so we can copy them and get out of here?"

This was not the response I was led to expect as a graduate student at Columbia University. I had envisioned a room full of students eagerly committing their thoughts to paper, relieved by and grateful for the opportunity to voice their own ideas. Where had I gone wrong? Why didn't my professors cover resistance in their methods courses? After using up several boxes of tissues as I contemplated my next move, I decided to write my students a letter in answer to their question. After all, they deserved to know why they were doing what they were doing and how writing could be a tool for them to have agency in their lives. When students arrived at class the following day, they received my letter, which made a passionate appeal for the power of writing to help us shape our world, and I instructed students that if they had problems with our class in the future, they needed to . . . put them in writing. Students read it, responded appreciatively, and our class moved on with a stronger sense of purpose.

I am often reminded of Thoreau's reflection "It is not enough to be busy; the question is, what are we busy about?" The outcomes of a socially just education are measured not in the content of the curriculum that students absorb (although this is certainly important), but in the ways in which students learn to become agents for justice and social good in their own lives and communities. A socially just education helps students to answer, and to live with, larger questions of agency: What does my learning help me do in the world? And how can I use my learning to make a difference?

Many teachers I've worked with over the years have expressed frustration at students'lack of independence—an essential move toward developing agency. They note that many students do not independently read, engage in learning work in the classroom, or manage their own discussions. In the classroom, we have worked on how to create conditions in which students can become more independent readers, writers, and thinkers—in the context of purposeful learning. Developing students' independence requires that we hand over responsibility for learning to them and that we gradually release, over time, the learning work in ways that enable students to apply their reading, writing, and thinking to new contexts while progressively increasing their roles and responsibilities in the learning process (Wood, Bruner, & Ross, 1976).

Students can develop agency, then, when we model for them how to read, write, speak, and think in ways that make a difference, give them opportunities to practice with guidance and support in the classroom, and create meaningful contexts for them to apply their skills and thinking work to their lives and communities in ways that effect positive changes for social good. Students become agents when we see them read texts and independently analyze how social status affects opportunities, make connections to their own lives and communities, and begin problem solving with one another about ways they can reimagine and reshape their social worlds for greater equity and justice. Figure 1.5 describes some features of classrooms where teachers purposefully develop students' agency.

ASSESSING YOUR SCHOOL AND CLASSROOM CONTEXT

The criteria outlined above attempt to create a vision for what is possible in high school classrooms that strive to enact socially just teaching and

Figure 1.5. Seeing Agency in Socially Just Classrooms

What Teachers Say and Do	What Students Say and Do
Provide authentic models or examples of how to use literacy skills to enact positive change in one's life or community	Make connections from their reading, writing, and learning to issues in their lives and communities
Create conditions and opportunities for students to read and write in ways that promote social action	Develop plans for how their learning can shape their actions and interactions with others
Help students study how others (especially members of students' racial, ethnic, socioeconomic, or cultural communities) act as agents to shape their lives and communities for social good	Engage with adults and students from their own and other communities as part of their learning experience
Create opportunities for learning that connect students to their home communities—and to other people outside their realm of experience	Independently apply the reading, writing, and thinking work they do in the classroom to new situations and contexts that benefit their lives and communities

learning. What goals might you want to set to move your own work forward? As a starting point, consider the following questions as a means to assess and reflect on the current state of teaching and learning in your classroom or school context.

Stance

- Who takes responsibility when students are not learning?
- Do students have ownership and responsibility over their learning?
- Do teachers and students work collaboratively in the classroom to construct meaning and work in ways that foster relationships of inclusivity, shared power, and respect?

Relevance

- Are all students actively and meaningfully engaged in their own learning?
- Do students spend the majority of instructional time in classrooms engaged in thinking?
- What is the evidence of students' thinking?
- What are students thinking about and how does their learning relate to their own lives, communities, and purposes?

Access

- How well do students understand the key concepts in their classes?
- How do they demonstrate and act on their understanding?
- How is the development of students' thinking supported in ways that help them gain access to challenging texts, ideas, and content?
- How well do students access the knowledge they are learning in their classrooms? How do their literacy skills (reading, writing, speaking, listening) affect their access to knowledge, and what role do teachers play in providing the kind of instruction that provides access?
- Do students understand what their learning gives them access to?

Identity

- What does students' engagement in school reflect about their identities as learners and human beings?
- What Discourses (about race, ethnicity, gender, socioeconomic status, learning, and opportunity) are enacted in the school and classroom?
- How does classroom interaction create a space for students to understand and discuss social identities and positions—and construct healthy identities and possibilities for themselves?

Agency

- How well do students independently use the skills and habits of thinking they are learning?
- How do they use their learning to make a difference in their lives and communities?
- When students don't understand, are they empowered to do something about it?
- To what extent do students participate in their school, classrooms, and community as democratic citizens empowered to shape the world around them?
- What is the nature and quality of students' interactions with others in those communities, and what issues of justice, inclusivity, and equity might we want to see transformed through our work with students?

The distance between the educational ideals outlined in this chapter—stance, relevance, access, identity, and agency—and the kinds of real class-rooms that work toward those ideals is the territory this book inhabits. What do inspiring classrooms look like in practical terms? And how, given the challenges facing schools and teachers today, do we make the ideal real? How do we enact socially just teaching as a means to meaningful, rigorous, and equitable learning for all students?

To that end, the succeeding chapters in this book address the following:

- How to build classroom communities that reflect socially just ideals
- How to develop student voice in the context of rigorous instruction in language arts
- How to develop students' ownership in learning through a personal inquiry approach
- How to observe and analyze social justice problems of practice in the teaching of reading
- Strategies for responding to problems of practice in the teaching of reading
- How to develop units of study for social justice
- Implications for socially just leadership

Having worked in numerous urban, suburban, and rural districts, I know many of the challenges facing teachers who strive for social justice in diverse contexts and in their everyday practice. Each chapter therefore offers possibilities and examples for how to navigate those challenges, provides a sample framework for instruction, and offers strategies, sample lessons, and examples of student work aimed at addressing the problems of practice at hand. The examples of classroom practice presented here were developed through my work as an educational consultant with teachers and students in diverse school districts, and I am indebted to those hardworking teachers who have engaged with me in the challenge of turning theory into practice. It is my hope that readers see here a glimpse of what is possible for socially just teaching and learning and how it might be done.

CHAPTER TWO

Building Better Classroom Communities

Putting Student Voices at the Center

TEACHING FOR SOCIAL JUSTICE begins with creating conditions in the classroom for all students to be successful learners and to have access to high-quality, relevant instruction. Because learning is social and occurs within the medium of language and social interaction, the kinds of classroom communities in which students engage have direct bearing on the quality and content of their learning. Powerful classroom communities steep students in a culture of thinking and intellectual engagement while fostering the skills and dispositions students need to participate in civic discourse, inquiry, and collaboration. Socially just teaching, then, must be concerned not only with creating equitable opportunities for learning but also with creating the conditions and supports students need to access those opportunities.

This chapter begins at the end: with a vision for high school classroom community and one example of what that might look like. From there, we work backward to consider the theories of learning that can inform what we teach about community and how we teach it, focusing on the structures and strategies that help to create conditions for learning in a culture of thinking. We will look at what students need to know and be able to do to become constructive members of a literate community. Finally, we will examine methods for developing a classroom culture of thinking in which students learn interdependence and agency.

A PORTRAIT OF COMMUNITY IN ALISSA NIEMI HEIKKILA'S CLASS

Alissa Niemi Heikkila's 10th-grade students gathered up front for a class meeting at the start of 4th period. The class was representative of the larger context of Mount Rainier High School, a comprehensive public high school where 49% of students were on free or reduced-price lunch and the student body reflected the rich racial and cultural diversity of the urban Seattle area.

On this day, students were working on reading projects designed around a thinking goal that each student had identified for his or her own growth as a reader. As part of their work, all students read a Shakespeare play of their choice and determined how they would demonstrate their progress by the end of the unit. Students' thinking goals varied. Some students, for example, had chosen to work on analyzing the relationships between certain characters in their play in order to infer themes. Other students had identified that they struggled with inferring tone through dialogue and word choice and opted to focus on how to better analyze those literary elements. Depending on students' goals, they needed to make a plan for their thinking work so that they could spend the majority of their class time engaged in rigorous, purposeful reading.

As Alissa began the class meeting, she posted the calendar to remind students when their notes and literary responses were due. Students listened with their notebooks open, recording information they needed to plan for their work that day. To support students' choices for independent work time, Alissa used an "If/Then" chart to help students determine their focus and to organize class time they would spend on reading work. An example of the chart is shown in Figure 2.1.

Once she had reviewed students' work choices for the day, Alissa used the following share session to develop the classroom community in ways that supported students' independence—and interdependence—for learning.

Figure 2.1. If/Then Chart for Supporting Students' Independent Work Time

If ...	Then ...
You haven't finished reading	Work on reading and taking notes in connection with your thinking goal
You haven't figured out what your final product will be	**Try:** Make a list of possibilities that fit with your thinking goal Reread and reflect on your notes—what are you already doing that could work well for your final product?
You're finished reading, and have an idea of what your final product for the unit will look like	Work on rereading your notes, figuring out what you'll use, and formatting (e.g., highlighting) according to what your final product might look like

Alissa: Is there anyone here who knows what their
    end product is going to look like? [*Several hands
    go up; Alissa calls on one student.*] So Jake, do
    you have an idea of what you want to do today,
    based on your end product?

Jake: Well, my notes are basically like . . . you
    know, when we did our first unit this year, we
    were looking for just three supporting things?
    Remember how we took a line in music, and
    analyzed it and had to defend it? I want to do
    that same thing, but with a whole section from
    Shakespeare.

> Notice how Alissa
> hands over the
> responsibility for
> decision making to
> Jake—and uses his
> work as an example
> to help other
> students consider
> possibilities for their
> own work.

Alissa: Okay. So you might want to revisit how you did your notes from that
    assignment help you.

Jake: Yeah. And then I'm going to use color coding to help with my
    organization by highlighting what fits with my idea.

Alissa: So Jake is making a plan for what his end product will look like.
    Some of you may just need to talk about it. Turn to the person next to
    you: What are you going to do today, given where you are in working on
    your thinking goal and final product?

At Alissa's prompting, students turned to discuss with one another their progress, the challenges
they faced in their academic work, and what supports they felt they needed to do their best. Every
student engaged in thoughtful academic planning.
Here, two student partners discuss their plans:

> Alissa routinely
> used partner talk to
> support students'
> independence *and*
> interdependence.
> Students often had
> opportunities to
> discuss the decisions
> they made about
> their own learning.

Carissa: I need to figure out more about how
    relationships change with the characters of Iago
    and Othello. I'm going to focus on that. What
    are you doing?

Miguel: I think I need to outline my presentation.
    I'm going to read the act summaries to help me revisit my notes.

Alissa: [*Signaling that students should stop partner talk and focus on her
    instruction*] Okay. Please wrap up your conversation. [*After another
    moment of conversation, students are quiet.*] So moving around, it sounds
    like a lot of you have a plan for today of what you need to do to reach
    your end goal. Is there anyone who's kind of stuck? And it's okay to be
    stuck. . . . [*A few students express hesitation.*] Let's hear some of your plans
    for end products to get some ideas. Leona had an epiphany. Leona, why
    don't you share your epiphany with the class?

Leona: I had a hard time figuring out what to do for my project. So I decided to get a long piece of paper and block out each character in Act 5 and what they would be doing, based on the whole tone and mood of Act 5.

Alissa creates a space for students to be "stuck" and to work collectively through challenges in their learning process.

Alissa: Great. So you're doing your interpretation on a bigger scale, but with a narrower focus now, by looking at the tone and mood that is created.

Leona: Yeah.

Alissa: Let's hear one more. Maria, what about you?

Maria: Well, I haven't really decided yet, but I'm thinking maybe a shorter essay that answers my thinking goal questions, or a process notebook.

Alissa: Let's see if we can help her out a bit. What's your thinking goal?

Maria: Well, I have a few different questions. One is about how Iago [from *Othello*] affects the other characters and why the characters give in to Iago. And how Iago affects the characters' relationships.

Alissa: Any advice for Maria on how her end product could demonstrate her goal?

Jose: Maybe a reflection. Like a process paper about what you were thinking as you were tracking Iago.

Alissa implicitly teaches students how to become interdependent. She uses whole-group discussion to engage in helping students solve problems in their learning.

Alissa: Okay. Any other ideas?

Indigo: Maybe something that shows both of his sides, like how he acts to Othello and then like the majority of the time how he acts to everyone else.

Ahmed: And maybe you could track the changes to his character, like what he was like when he started and how he was at the end.

Alissa: Like noticing shifts in the character?

Ahmed: Yeah.

Alissa: Do any of those sound good to you?

Maria: Yeah. They sound good.

Alissa: So in your notes today, you might want to take on some of those ideas. Okay?

Maria: Yeah.

Alissa: [*To the group*] So if you're stuck getting started, stay up front here so I can check in with you. Otherwise, have a productive class period.

[*Students get up from the seminar area at the front of the classroom and return to their seats. Inside of 2 minutes, they are busy reading and writing.*]

While this is but a snapshot of what a literate community can look and sound like in a high school classroom, several things are striking about the culture of learning that Alissa and her students have created. Unlike in many high school classrooms, students are active participants in the classroom and engage in thinking about and planning for their own learning. They clearly have ownership in the community and in their learning work. Alissa's students know what they are learning and why—and their work in the classroom supports rigorous reading, writing, and intellectual engagement with texts and with one another. Notions of community are not just warm and fuzzy concepts; they are grounded in the serious work of learning. In the following sections, we'll look at how this classroom community came to be through Alissa's careful instruction.

WHAT STUDENTS NEED TO KNOW AND BE ABLE TO DO IN A CLASSROOM COMMUNITY THAT SUPPORTS SOCIAL JUSTICE WORK

I remember once when I observed my 10-year-old son, Ben, brushing his teeth as he got ready for bed. It had been a while since I'd needed to supervise his tooth brushing, and I assumed all was proceeding in a thorough and efficient manner. Much to my dismay, I witnessed the toothbrush lazily glossed over the front teeth then wiggled absentmindedly inside his mouth while he spent the majority of the time making faces at himself in the mirror. Panicking, I tried to remember the date of his last dental appointment and calculate the likelihood of finding a cavity on the next visit. I thought he knew how to brush his teeth correctly; what happened? Hoping to stave off any cavities that might be brewing, I intervened, demonstrated the correct way to reach and brush all of the teeth, coached him a bit as he tried a "re-do," and praised his efforts. I also planned to start checking up on him every night to make sure his "practice" formed a habit. The cavity crisis had been averted, at least momentarily.

As with many things, our beliefs about what kids *should* know how to do often get in the way of seeing what they *actually* do in practice and what they need to know in order to do what we are asking. Behaving as thoughtful, respectful participants in a learning community may seem, to those of us who have done it as adults for a good while, to be as natural and obvious as breathing or drinking coffee in the morning. Yet many of our students have been silenced in school, rather than invited to participate; many have learned to listen for the teacher's ideas rather than develop their own; many have experienced classrooms as places with rules to passively follow rather than as places where they actively make and negotiate meanings. In short, we cannot expect students to fulfill a socially just vision of a literate community if they do not know what such a community looks like or how to engage in it. If we want students to learn to engage in a culture of thinking and to form habits for engagement in civic discourse and learning, then we must explicitly demonstrate the literate behavior we want to see. With this goal in mind, we can then provide daily opportunities for students to practice intentional engagement in classroom community and continually coach and monitor their progress toward the kind of learners we want them to become.

The work of participation in a literate community must therefore be defined for students in order for them to learn the discourses and ways of being (what Gee, 1999, calls Discourses) necessary to engage in a literate and democratic community. In order to establish a classroom culture that nourishes active thinking and civic participation, students need to know what knowledge and skills they are being taught and expected to demonstrate. They also need models of the kinds of discourses and behaviors that characterize such a community. With a shared vision in mind, teachers can then provide ongoing coaching, support, and feedback on students' practice of the knowledge and skills they are in the process of learning.

Figure 2.2 offers a vision for what a culture of thinking looks like in practice and outlines the knowledge and skills needed for participation in classroom communities that support socially just teaching and learning. Depending on a given group of students and the context in which they learn, Figure 2.2 can serve as a starting point for assessment and analysis: What knowledge and skills do students demonstrate through their class discussion, participation, and behavior? Do they demonstrate an understanding of the purpose for classroom community and what it can look and sound like? At the beginning of the year, we might consider identifying a core group of three to five concepts and skills about community that we want to explicitly teach to and expect students to learn and demonstrate during the first 4 to 6 weeks of school. Teaching for a literate community is ongoing work, though, and requires that we continually assess, monitor, instruct, and support students in developing the habits and skills we want to see.

If, for example, students struggle as a group with merely engaging in actively learning in the classroom and are hesitant to share their own thinking, this would be a critical area for instructional focus, as many of the other skills of community membership and learning rely on active participation. As we examine how Alissa and other teachers have taught their students to become a community, we will consider various strategies for approaching problems of practice we can encounter with real kids.

Figure 2.2. Knowledge and Skills for Engaging in Classroom Community

Students Need to Know	Students Need to be Able to Do
Members of a learning community play an active role in the learning process: They share their thinking, seek understanding, and take responsibility for furthering and supporting their own learning as well as the learning of the group.	Focus and refocus classroom talk on learning, even when it veers off course. Actively read, listen, and share their thinking about what they are learning. Initiate new questions, research, or reading. Provide evidence to support or complicate their own ideas or the ideas of others.
Empowered learners have a voice in deciding the purpose for their learning and what they will "do" with it. Community members use their learning to accomplish something beyond the classroom walls.	Use their developing literacy skills (reading, writing, speaking, and thinking) to do meaningful work in the world: communicate ideas, initiate projects that matter, improve their lives and communities, and take a stand on matters that affect them or harm others.
Members of a learning community are accountable for accurate sources of knowledge shared in the community.	Understand, refer to, and represent knowledge and ideas presented in the texts and materials studied for the class with thoroughness and accuracy.
Participants in a learning community are accountable for listening to, understanding, and responding to the ideas of others in the community.	Understand, refer to, and represent the ideas of others. Contribute to the development of a line of thinking in classroom conversations by adding to, extending, or complicating the thinking and ideas being constructed through classroom discourse.
Members of a learning community are accountable for the habits of thinking and reasoning that characterize their field of study.	Name, engage in, and assess the quality of their thinking work in the classroom, given the habits of reasoning and thinking that are explicitly taught and developed.
Learning communities are purposeful: Members know what they are learning, why they are learning it, and how their daily work relates to these larger objectives.	Make thoughtful decisions about what they are learning and why. Make intentional choices about how to engage in learning, given their explicit purpose.
Members of the learning community understand that they are part of an inclusive democracy: They engage in civic discussion and debate, make shared decisions, and treat one another with equity, dignity, and respect.	Participate actively and respectfully in collaborative meaning making, discussion, and decision making. Debate ideas without demeaning people. Listen and respond to the ideas of others, assessing and questioning their own ideas alongside the thinking of others.
Members of the learning community draw from their own cultures and funds of knowledge in constructing the culture of the classroom. Participants recognize, honor, negotiate, and coexist with the cultural beliefs, values, and practices of others in the community. They understand that they are engaged in building the knowledge and understanding of a unique learning community through their relationships with one another.	Recognize and reflect on the limits of their own experiences and perspectives and demonstrate intellectual generosity and fallibility through revision of thinking.

CREATING CONDITIONS FOR LEARNING TO THINK AS A MEMBER OF A LITERATE COMMUNITY

Alissa taught the knowledge and skills of developing a socially just community while using the workshop structure (Atwell, 1998; Plaut, 2009) to design a learning environment that was both communal and independence-oriented. Her use of workshop structure accommodated a wide range of students' interests, choices, and ways of working. In a workshop model, instructional time follows a fairly predictable structure, beginning with a seminar-style lesson (or "mini-lesson") during which time students gather in a circle to engage in learning a lesson focused on a new concept, processes, or strategies for reading, writing, or thinking, or to discuss their work for the day (in the preceding example from Alissa's classroom, students participated in what is referred to as a "status-of-the-class conference"). The heart of a workshop classroom is time devoted to students working independently or collaboratively in partners or small groups to engage in reading, writing, and thinking work.

On the day we observed, Alissa's students worked independently to do the following: They read a Shakespeare play of their choice, used thinking goals to guide their reading and learning, took notes on the text that related to their goals, monitored and planned for the summative project that would reflect their progress, and met with other students and Alissa as needed to get support. Students purposefully and independently engaged in reading and writing for 45 minutes while Alissa met with individual students to confer; during this time she assessed their progress as readers and thinkers and provided coaching to raise the level of their work. Alissa reserved the last 10 minutes of instructional time for a "share session," in which she invited students to discuss, as a whole group, the thinking work they had done that day.

Alissa's strategic use of the workshop structure helped her to create the conditions for learning that Cambourne (1995) identified in his study of young children's language acquisition. While these conditions have been applied specifically to language learning, I wish to apply them to the work of teaching students what they need to know and be able to do in order to engage in a literate community in the classroom. The conditions, when intentionally created through classroom instruction, increase the likelihood that students will learn how to form the basis of a viable, inclusive learning community.

Cambourne's Conditions: From Theory to Practice

In each of the following sections, I outline how Cambourne's conditions apply to students' literacy learning and to the work of building community. Using strategies developed by Alissa and others, I will also illustrate ways to create each condition in the classroom.

Immersion. Learners independently develop and apply literacy skills when they are immersed daily in reading, writing, and thinking work with texts of all kinds. In a workshop classroom, immersion happens not only through lessons and demonstrations but also through daily independent practice in reading, writing, and thinking.

Similarly, students require immersion in community routines and processes that support social justice work in order to become proficient members of a literate community. Because routines help to create habits for thinking and interacting, teachers must carefully design what they want students' talk and interactions to look and sound like in the classroom on an ongoing basis. Routines often need to be explicitly taught and named in order for immersion to happen in a meaningful way. Because students can come to the classroom taking a passive rather than an active stance, some teachers I've worked with have found that they need to clarify for students how classroom time will be used inside the workshop structure, what role they expect students to play, and why these roles matter for developing students' agency. Some teachers have found it helpful, for example, to create class charts to define their expectations for students' roles in a workshop. Once the roles have been explicitly introduced and discussed, students often need consistent coaching and feedback in order to naturally take on these roles independently. Figure 2.3 shows an example of this kind of learning support chart.

Alissa capitalized on the routine of daily share sessions as a means to foster both independence and interdependence. As part of the workshop structure, the share session provides a purposeful space during the class period for students to develop their identities as community members because the teacher crafts this time to collectively reflect on, extend, and problem solve around students' learning. Alissa's students identified class share sessions and meetings as important to developing their learning and collaboration. In a year-end reflection, one student wrote that "community meetings forced us to face our class/group issues and what we liked and needed out of the class." At times, Alissa used the workshop structure flexibly, beginning class with a community meeting or share session in order to raise issues or build on the previous day's work. As a means to immerse students in the work of learning to become community members, Alissa used the share session to create teachable moments focused on instruction—and on continually reflecting: How are things working for us as learners? What can we do to improve?

Demonstration. Learners need demonstrations—from the teacher and other learners—of how texts and ideas are constructed, interpreted, and used. In a culture of thinking, students may at times serve as models for one another. The

Figure 2.3. Teaching Workshop Structure to Build Classroom Community

Your Role (Student)	My Role (Teacher)
Mini-lesson/Seminar	
Sit next to your partner	Set the purpose for the day
Share your thinking (say something relevant and explain)	Explain the focus of our learning for the day and model how to do the thinking work
Listen to instruction and take notes	
Ask questions and share your thinking	Create opportunities for you to think about what we're learning (talking or writing) and ask questions
Listen—be a good community member	
Share what you need for your own learning	Listen, respond to, and coach your thinking to help support your understanding of the lesson
Make a plan for your learning for the day	
	Help you plan for independent work time
Independent Work Time	
Be clear in your purpose for the day—have a plan	Confer with you to learn more about your learning process and to coach you in your thinking/reading/writing
Make decisions about how you will use your time for learning and what resources you need	Raise issues of relevance to the whole group
Use all your time for learning work (reading, writing, thinking, discussion)	Maintain a productive work environment
Maintain a productive work environment	
Share	
Share your understanding, thinking, and work with a partner, small group, or whole group	Share observations/issues noted during independent work time
Post your thinking or group work	Further our collective understanding of the concepts/strategies we're working on
Raise questions or issues related to your learning	
Make connections to the mini-lesson and to ongoing work	Facilitate discussion that helps you make good decisions about your learning
Take notes as needed	Synthesize, extend, and push our collective thinking forward
Listen to and learn from the contributions of other community members	Listen
	Set the stage for our ongoing work

teaching of literate and intellectual skills, strategies, and processes is direct and explicit so that students know what they are being taught and expected to do.

Similarly, students need some direct instruction in how to develop an interdependent and inclusive community; this becomes part of the content that is taught. Here demonstration includes explicit instruction (how to) and teacher modeling of the kinds of discourse and practices that characterize strong communities. While it may be surprising to think that high school students—after 10 or more years of school—need direct instruction in how to be students in a classroom community, I have found time and time again that this is exactly the case with many students I have worked with in a variety of school contexts. In a culture defined by rugged individualism, many students come to the classroom with limited experiences or models of what powerful community engagement can look or sound like.

Building more powerful communities requires that as teachers we take risks to be vulnerable with students by modeling our own literate lives and ways of interacting in community. In a socially just paradigm, teachers position themselves as part of the classroom community, not separate from it. But they also leverage their expertise to help students acquire more sophisticated skills for thinking, speaking, and interacting.

To create the condition of demonstration, teachers model the kind of role as community member that they expect of students. What requires modeling depends largely on what aspects of community need further instruction and support. Teachers might need to demonstrate, for example, how to disagree re-spectfully, or how to push one another's thinking in productive ways. Because demonstrations are most powerful when they are explicit, I have found in my work with teachers that it can be helpful for students to specifically name the kinds of moves we want them to see in a demonstration. For example, if a teacher and I wanted to help students better respond to and follow up on one another's ideas, we might demonstrate (together) the kind of conversation we want to hear. Students could then help to co-construct a chart to name the kinds of things they can say and do to improve their collective work. Such a chart might be structured as follows in Figure 2.4.

To develop students' interdependence and ownership, we can ask them to model the habits of speaking and interacting we want to cultivate in the classroom community. If members of a small group of students, for example, do a nice job of working to challenge one another's thinking, the teacher can have that group share—or demonstrate—their process for the larger class. When possible, this strategy has the advantage of creating a stronger sense of ownership among students for the work of building community.

Engagement. Engagement is essential for learning to take place. In a culture of thinking, students feel capable, purposeful, and safe; the teacher

Figure 2.4. How to Support and Push One Another's Thinking in the Community

Things We Can Do	Things We Can Say
Paraphrase the other person's idea to make sure we've understood their thinking.	So it sounds like you're saying . . .
	[Name] is making a point that . . .
Ask follow-up questions to clarify.	What do you mean by . . . ?
	Can you explain . . . ?
Identify which parts of the person's idea you agree and disagree with— and explain your position. Use "I" statements.	I agree with what you said about ____.
	However, I disagree about ____ because . . .
	I don't see enough evidence to support ____ because . . .
Focus on the *idea*, not the *person*. What part of the reasoning or evidence does not seem valid?	____ doesn't make sense to me because . . .

actively and persistently works to foster inclusiveness and belonging while making sure that students have enough instructional support to take on the intellectual work of the class. The teacher uses strategies like partner talk or reflective writing to ensure that every student is actively engaged in learning and feels a sense of belonging in the community.

For students who are resistant learners or who are socially marginalized or vulnerable, the teacher must work strategically and directly to engage them. "I begin the year by breaking down how students see each other," Alissa explained, noting that she worked to help students "see each other differently" by positioning each student as a resource in the classroom. Students' responses (including notes from their discussions, student work, and observations of students' conversations and interactions) served as a site for instruction and nurturing. Alissa actively validated and named students' thinking work and what they were doing well. "This had to be consistent, though, or it wouldn't work," she added. During community meetings and share sessions, she strategically shifted power in the classroom by sharing a variety of students' work and focused on bringing forward and valuing the work and ideas of students who were less visible or marginalized. Because multiple voices were brought forward and validated, students developed identities as contributing community members and came to see each other as valuable assets and colleagues.

Expectation. Every student is expected to think and use his or her mind well in a classroom culture of thinking. The teacher sets the tone that active engagement in thinking is "what we do here as members of this community." Classroom structures and routines, such as beginning the class period and mini-lesson with students gathered in a close-knit circle for instruction and discussion, create expectations for engagement as well. In Alissa's classroom, students could not hide in the back row—there was no back row.

Expectations are communicated implicitly through the design of the classroom environment, the teacher's stance, and the ways in which students' roles are structured during learning. They are also communicated, more subtly, by what we will and will not accept from students in terms of their discourse, work, and ways of interacting. When expectations create a continual site of struggle, I find I need to reflect on what I accept from students and where the "apple" may not be falling far from the "tree." We cannot merely state expectations in the classroom; for students to learn expectations requires modeling of the desired behavior, as well as continual explanation and follow-up, particularly for struggling students. Not all marginalized students, for example, jump at the chance to "work harder," especially when they may have learned and got by with low expectations for much of their school career. When students hold lower expectations for themselves than we do, they may need us to help them learn why they should care in the first place. In a socially just classroom, students can begin to see themselves as competent, valuable learners. While expectations originate from the teacher, they must ultimately be owned by the learning community if they are to be meaningful for students. When students are taught to value one another as resources for learning, they can begin to hold higher expectations for themselves and their classmates as well. This takes consistency, persistence, and time.

Responsibility. Ownership and engagement are increased when learners have opportunities to make choices and decisions about their own learning. This requires teachers to not only outline the parameters of the learning work in which they want students to engage but also to facilitate students' decision making about what parts of their reading, writing, and thinking work to take on during the learning process, as well as how and when to do so. In Alissa's class, students were given the responsibility of setting goals for their reading and thinking work and for determining how best to demonstrate progress toward those goals. Prior to creating these expectations, Alissa had immersed students in the reading of Shakespearean texts and had demonstrated how to navigate challenging text and read with a particular lens or purpose. This critical step better ensured that students could actually do the work she asked to them to take on independently.

During share sessions and community meetings, Alissa also helped students to develop a monitoring role by raising questions and issues for the class. Students learned to identify where their community needed to be stronger and were given the responsibility—and tools—for collective problem solving. Alissa asked, and taught students to ask, "We see a problem in our community, so what are we going to do about it?" Through facilitation and dialogue, she helped students learn to take responsibility for one another—and to be constructive rather than competitive. In one class, for example, several students noted that not everyone was participating and they raised the issue as a community problem to solve. As Alissa watched, the class came up with strategies they could use to include one another and support students who were more reluctant to share. That moment proved to be a powerful turning point for the class, when their collective action revealed the power of community to change students' experiences in school.

Practice/use. In a socially just classroom, students' ideas, discourse, and learning work is always at the center of the classroom and drives the purpose of daily instruction. Learners need time and opportunity to practice and use their developing reading, writing, and thinking skills in meaningful and purposeful ways. Without practice and use, teachers cannot measure or assess students' learning. For this reason, independent work time is the heart of the workshop structure, for it enables instruction to support students' transfer of learning.

Classroom communities cannot develop without meaningful practice in authentic, purposeful, and communal work. And students cannot practice building a better community if they do not know what, specifically, they are practicing. When students in Alissa's class engaged in partner work, group work, or shared class discussion, she often specifically named what they did well in their efforts to work together. At other times, she named explicitly what the group needed to practice. She would say, "We've done a nice job of making sure that many different voices are being heard in the classroom. Yesterday, for example, Serena invited LaToya to share and we all benefited from the ideas she shared. We still need to work on elaborating on our ideas, though, so today I'd like us to practice asking each other follow-up questions as we try to extend our thinking as a group." Community learning and discussions, therefore, were purposefully framed as part of the knowledge and skills that students were expected to develop.

Approximation. In the course of trying on the reading, writing, and thinking work of the class, students need permission to experiment, to make mistakes, and to rehearse their thinking without fear of getting "the wrong answer." While accountability to accuracy and to standards of reasoning are important and valued in the learning community, students know that "being stuck" and making mistakes are essential parts of the learning process. Effective teachers coach students in the act of learning by building on and teaching into students' approximations.

This is also true of learning how to think and act in a classroom community. When teachers observe how students are talking and interacting as a group, they can consider: What have I taught and expected students to do as members of a learning community? How does the behavior I see reflect what they are learning about how to engage in a learning community? Recognizing students' approximations helps us to see the work of community engagement as a process that takes time and continuous support.

Feedback/response. In a rigorous culture of thinking, students receive response to their reading, writing, and thinking work from what Cambourne (1995) calls "more knowledgeable others" (p. 187). When response is relevant, appropriate, timely, and nonthreatening, students can better name what they have learned and what more they need to work on. I have found at times that when students do *not* receive this kind of response, their engagement in learning falters. They may think, "Why should I bother working so hard when no one ever reads or comments on my work?" And they would be right to question.

In a socially just classroom, students' ideas, discourse, and learning work is always at the center of the classroom and drives the purpose of daily instruction. Students receive daily response to their work in a variety of ways. Effective mini-lessons can focus on the assessed needs of the class and provide an explicit purpose for the day's learning. Alissa often began class by showing examples of student work, naming what students did well, and noting areas for growth that would be addressed through the day's lesson. Often these areas also related to things they needed to work on as a classroom community.

During independent work time, Alissa responded to students' individual and communal work through conferring and during her facilitation of small groups. Learning issues she uncovered during independent work time could then be brought to the whole class for discussion to forward the learning.

Finally, Alissa created conditions for students to act as "more knowledgeable others" who could offer feedback and response as well. At various times throughout the year, students engaged in small-group community meetings to discuss what was working well in the classroom, what they liked, what they needed, and where they got stuck. Alissa used students' feedback to then inform her next steps and instructional decisions for the class in ways that made students feel listened to and valued.

In order for students' literate discourse, interactions, and behaviors to constitute a socially just culture of thinking, they need to be immersed in the work of becoming an authentic community, receive demonstrations of what it looks and sounds like to be a member of such a community, be expected and taught to engage frequently in the desired behaviors and work of the group, have responsibility for the culture that is built, and explicitly practice and receive feedback on the kinds of discourse, habits of thinking, and literate behaviors they are expected to learn. The work of teaching students how to participate in a culture of thinking as a member of a literate community is always a shadow curriculum that supports the ongoing reading, writing, and thinking work of the classroom—regardless of the content being taught.

On Stance

As we can see, teachers play a critical role in designing classroom communities that create conditions for social justice learning. The way the teacher positions him/herself within that community, however, plays an important part as well. When teachers prioritize students and their needs over the content of a given lesson or topic, when they hand over some control to students in the classroom and allow them to make mistakes as part of the process of learning to work together, they assume a stance that empowers students as individuals and community members. Alissa explained, "Stance is so important. . . . I take a position where I am not answering all of the students' questions, throwing things back at them and requiring them to talk to each other. As a teacher, you're taking a risk . . . by providing space for kids to figure things out together." Community cannot be explicitly taught or learned unless we position (and require) students to have more power, agency, and purposeful collaboration.

How does our stance affect and engage students? When asked to reflect on what helped their learning in Alissa's class, her students mentioned many things that illustrate how they perceived her stance as one that required and expected their active engagement. Students noticed how her questions turned the responsibility for learning back onto them when she asked questions such as the following:

- What in the text makes you think this?
- What did you take as a person from this reading and discussion?
- Why do you think this? What else can we take from this idea?
- Whose ideas or contributions in class today helped you with your own thinking?

Students acknowledged that moves like these had trained them to be on their toes when Alissa worked with them during class time. They recognized that the way in which learning was structured helped them attempt more of the work on their own and with partners. One student wrote on his reflection that "if we were timid, you would work with us personally and use the same methods slowly and simply, but not let us get away with slacking." In a socially just classroom environment, students need this kind of unwavering intellectual press and support in order to engage individually and collectively with rigorous learning. The student body at Mount Rainier High School, where Alissa taught the lesson presented earlier, encompassed a diverse range of backgrounds and skills. Yet it was difficult to distinguish the advantaged and disadvantaged students in Alissa's class because all students were engaged—and were treated as important, capable, and contributing members of the community.

ASSESSING YOUR LEARNERS AND CHOOSING A FOCUS

While workshop structures and routines create conditions for learning by affording daily time for demonstration in the mini-lesson, responsibility and practice in the independent work time, and response during the share session, our stance within that structures matters greatly. Alissa's language, approach, and classroom routines helped to construct an inclusive academic community where all students were expected to succeed and received the support to do so.

As with many things, teaching students to develop the knowledge and skills needed to work successfully with each other in the classroom requires an ongoing process of practice and reflection.

Using the criteria outlined in Figure 2.2 and the conditions for learning, reflect on the community you are trying to build in your own school or classroom. The following questions can help you identify what conditions may already be in place and which ones may need further explicit development:

- Have students been *immersed* in explicit and predictable routines that support the kind of community you want to see?
- Do students know, explicitly, why it is important to belong to a community and what a strong community looks and sounds like? Have they received *demonstrations or models* of the ways of speaking and interacting that characterize a literate and socially just community?
- How well are (all) students *engaged* in the learning community? If they are disengaged, how might the presence (or absence) of the other conditions for learning be affecting their engagement?
- How have *expectations* for the learning community been communicated and to what extent do students themselves own those expectations?
- Have conditions been created for students to *practice* meaningful work as a community every day?
- How is *approximation* named and valued as students take on the work of building classroom community? Do students feel safe making mistakes in the classroom?
- How have students received *feedback* on their roles as members of the classroom community? Has the response been relevant, timely, appropriate, and nonthreatening?

- Examine your own stance in the learning community. How might your role, including your language and interactions with students, be contributing to the dynamics you seek to improve?

As I have worked with teachers over the years to develop classroom communities, I have invariably found that building the vision for a socially just community requires patient focus and effort. I know few adults who can easily meet these criteria. Were such adult communities more present in our schools, I believe that students might more easily achieve them through the power of modeling alone. In schools committed to a vision for socially just teaching and learning, I encourage the adults to work toward these ideals in their collaboration with one another as part of the process of establishing strong communities in the classroom. The experience of building and belonging to an interdependent and inclusive community can have powerful, long-ranging effects in shaping students' vision for what kind of a world is possible, and what they want to build.

CHAPTER THREE

The Right to Their Own Ideas

Socially Just Classrooms Thrive on Students' Voices

"Dialogue is a moment where humans meet to reflect on their reality as they make and remake it."

—Paolo Freire & Ira Shor, "What is the 'Dialogical Method' of Teaching?," p. 13

MY COLLEAGUE, DOUG TUCKMAN, shared the following story with me. As a district literacy coach, he was working with a teacher in an 11th-grade language arts class. The teacher, Geoff, had noticed that students participated minimally in classroom discussion and that when they did talk, their responses tended to be perfunctory, as if they were hoping to end the conversation as quickly as possible. Geoff and Doug wanted to hear more voices and ideas in the room. In an effort to develop student discussion, they worked together on several lessons to help students share and grow their ideas about the texts they read.

On the first day, the lesson blew up. Several students stood up in protest, complaining that they were being asked to share their thinking, something they were not often asked to do as "regular track" students. "Teachers always say they want you to share your thinking, then they tell you what to think anyway. They don't really want you to share your own ideas—just come up with the answer," one student complained. These students were passionate—angry, even, at the teacher's attempt to change the game of school after they'd spent so many years passively mastering their silent and passive role. Asked suddenly to share their own thoughts and ideas, they became threatened by the game change.

I tell this story because the work of creating a culture of thinking can be challenging for many reasons, and there are important lessons we may need to learn and teach along the way. The story illustrates what is at stake when students experience low expectations for voicing their thoughts and ideas in the classroom. Rather than becoming independent and critical thinkers, students in many cases learn instead to absorb and recite the thinking of their teachers.

The previous chapters have focused on defining a framework for socially just teaching and on outlining ways to develop classroom communities aligned to that framework. But what happens inside these classroom communities—the kinds of thinking and talk that are engendered, supported, and explicitly taught—creates the intellectual culture that enables powerful learning to occur. Bomer and Bomer (2001) note, "Discourse creates thinking; indeed, it is the only source from which thinking derives" (p. 26). In classrooms where learning occurs inextricably within the medium of language, the quality of student talk (discourse) is therefore crucial; without the habits of thinking and discursive practice that characterize a high-functioning, literate, intellectual community, structures and curriculum alone create an empty shell.

This chapter therefore focuses on ways to develop the quality of student thinking in socially just classrooms by teaching students how to discuss their ideas about texts. Why is this important for socially just teaching? Picture this: As a teacher, you want students to engage in critical thinking about a story they are reading—say, *The Absolutely True Diary of a Part-Time Indian*, by Sherman Alexie (2007). You want to use the text to help students explore ideas about race, class, and gender and to consider the impacts of poverty on people's lives and possibilities. You read some of the text aloud to students, inviting them to respond, and you hear . . . crickets. Or maybe you hear the same four voices over and over, doing most of the thinking work of the class. Maybe you have begun a unit in which students are reading books in literature circles, but you find their ability to discuss their texts independently to be very limited, even though you have carefully chosen texts that you hope will engage students in reading about ideas connected to social justice. How do we actively engage all students in ways that ensure active, critical reading and thinking—and help them build a respectful culture of thinking where diverse voices and ideas might be heard? This chapter focuses on ways to explicitly teach and coach students in learning the skills and habits needed to participate in a literate culture of thinking.

Good classroom conversation is essential to the notion of literacy as a civil right (Greene, 2008). Not only does classroom discourse have the potential to create space for diverse student voices, but students' learning benefits greatly from rich classroom talk as well. Nystrand and Gamoran's (1991) research found that quality classroom discourse had a strong positive effect on students' learning when quality was defined by time devoted to discussion, the proportion of authentic questions from students, and the proportion of uptake (e.g., follow-up questions; Nystrand, 1997; Nystrand & Gamoran, 1991). Using Cambourne's conditions for learning as outlined in Chapter 2, the research illustrates that students need time to practice discussion, ask questions, and have teachers who listen and respond to their thinking in ways that further their ability to engage in high-level conversation. When these conditions are present, students are more likely to engage and learn.

Getting all students to talk about their thinking, especially in relation to the ideas in texts and the ideas of others, supports students' development as democratic citizens. The classroom can serve as an important arena for students to become contributing members to the world of ideas, to engage with diverse ways of thinking and being, and to become part of a civic life in which ideas are publicly examined and negotiated. To create the conditions for high-quality student talk and engagement, we must teach several important things: (1) what a good discussion looks and sounds like; (2) how to engage in good, text-based discussions; and (3) how to develop the quality of student thinking through discussion. But first we have to get all students talking. We can then assess their reading and thinking by examining the quality of their ideas and thinking processes in order to target instruction that helps them increasingly read and think at higher levels. When all students have these opportunities and expectations, we have begun the work of creating more equitable access for learning and intellectual engagement.

GETTING THEM ALL TALKING: CREATING STRUCTURES FOR TALK AND TEACHING THE SKILLS OF DISCUSSION

In my years as a middle and high school teacher, I never encountered a class that didn't need to learn how to do discussion. In a world where we interact with more people than ever before, and very often through screens, students (and adults) can at times struggle to master the art of conversation. Some students, too, come to the classroom with years of experience as passive listeners, having learned that the role of the student is to listen to the teacher rather than to construct his or her own meaning and ideas. Socially just teaching can target this problem by explicitly teaching, demonstrating, and coaching students in how to have equitable and rigorous discussions, helping students to analyze their own discussions in order to improve them, and creating many opportunities for practice. The ideas presented here can be used to create routines for discussion early in the year or can become the basis for a unit of study focused explicitly on developing better ideas through discussion.

Structures and Routines for Talk

To begin, we need to create structures that routinely engage students in learning-based discussion. Powerful student talk works as an engine to drive socially just, student-centered classrooms, but it cannot be left to chance; effective teachers manage student talk to promote deeper understanding and critical thinking. In part, managing talk effectively requires strategic use of different structures to facilitate discussion, including partner talk, small-group discussion, and whole-group discussion. Each structure can best be used for different purposes, as explained in Figure 3.1.

Figure 3.1. Ways to Structure Student Talk

Use partner talk to

- create opportunities for every student to rehearse thinking
- support and assess students' understanding throughout a lesson (beginning, middle, and end)
- rehearse skills and routines for discussion as a scaffold to having students work in small groups

Use small-group discussion to

- have students combine or synthesize their ideas from partner discussions
- divide topics, materials, or texts into small chunks to maximize the benefit of learning from other groups
- support student choices for reading and learning, as in the use of literature circles

Use whole-group discussion to

- establish a thread of common understanding about an idea or concept
- build on students' thinking and understanding by raising issues or ideas generated in partner or small-group discussions
- create accountability for partner and small-group discussions by requiring students to share thinking with the whole class

To scaffold students' learning of discussion skills, it is sometimes useful to focus on first using partner talk well before trying to develop small- or whole-group discussion. Some teachers find it helpful to create a predictable routine for talk initially by establishing student partnerships that remain fixed for a while until students become more comfortable and fluent sharing their thinking. Once students become more actively involved in discussion, it may become important to mix up the partnerships so that students have opportunities to learn from other thinkers.

Using the above structures is not enough, however. We can certainly ask students to talk to partners or in small groups, only to hear them blurt out a one-sentence response, maybe listening to one another—maybe not—then stop. Or we may hear them busy talking, but not in ways that focus and support their learning. Once the preceding routines and structures are in place, students need a clear picture of what a good discussion looks and sounds like, and they need explicit coaching and practice in the work of developing discussion. This is a matter of not only defining what good discussion behavior entails but also providing models, whenever possible, of engaged discussion about ideas and texts.

Defining What Good Literary Discussion Looks and Sounds Like

To start, we need to explicitly name the literate behavior we want to see and hear if we hope to see students practice it. I have found this to be an important move in clarifying expectations for students and give permission for them to take risks in sharing their ideas. Often I hear students explicitly ask me whether they can ask questions and say what they think. Because students have different histories of participation with class discussion in school, our efforts to make a safe and nurturing environment must create a level playing field for all kids to talk.

We can use a criteria chart such as that in Figure 3.2 to help students understand what we are looking and listening for as part of their collaborative work in the classroom. While a chart alone is not sufficient for teaching students to engage in better discussions, posting visual guidelines during the

Figure 3.2. A Sample Chart for Teaching Discussion

What Makes a Good Discussion?

In a good discussion, we leave our conversation with new ways of thinking about what we're reading and learning. We don't have to have answers to be good discussion members; rather, when we discuss our thinking, we explore ideas together. Here are some qualities that define a good discussion:

Looks Like	Sounds Like
Participants demonstrate active listening 　Eye contact 　Turning toward the speaker *Taking turns* *Using the text to support ideas* *Building on one another's ideas*	*Responding to the text* 　I noticed . . . 　I wonder . . . 　I didn't understand . . . 　I connected to . . . 　I inferred . . . *Responding to other readers* 　What did you mean by . . . ? 　Can you explain . . . ? 　In response to what ＿ said . . . 　I'd like to add . . . *Using the text to support thinking* 　[Part of the text] fits/doesn't fit with that idea because . . . 　On page ＿ / line ＿ it says [＿], 　which made me think . . .

early stages of teaching the routines and habits of discussion can help to provide scaffolding for students as they try on the "moves" of academic discourse and interaction. This provides teachers and students with a starting point and a means to assess their discussions and set goals for growth.

Early lessons in teaching the skills of discussion should focus on getting students to practice these moves and become comfortable getting their voices in the room. As students practice, we also need structured ways to monitor, assess, and respond to the discussion moves they take on. We can monitor students' participation using a chart like that in Figure 3.3 to name and record the moves students make in conversation. The chart can also serve as a means for classroom research and assessment. For this reason, I introduce the chart, explaining to students that we'll be working on practicing the discussion moves identified in the mini-lesson and explaining that my role will be to facilitate and study what students are doing by marking my observations on the chart. Students themselves play the most critical role: Their job, both individually and collectively, is to generate their own discussion based on their responses to a text we're reading together.

After trying on discussion for the first few class sessions, I then use Figure 3.3 to help students identify what they did well and what they need to work on. Part of the art of literary conversation involves monitoring, assessing, and responding to a discussion as it unfolds; these opportunities to debrief class discussions help students develop the metacognitive skills to better direct their own thinking through conversation. Eventually, students benefit from playing the role of class researchers as well. When students take on the work of naming the thinking work of their own discussions, the class becomes better empowered, collectively, to collaborate and improve.

Beginning Guided Practice with Reading and Discussion

When introducing discussion work, we want all students to actively read and have access to the same text. A short text (two to three pages) is ideal; poetry also works well. Once the focus on discussion skills has been introduced in a mini-lesson, it is important to give students copies of the text to mark. We can then read the text aloud, pausing at key moments to allow them to jot down responses to the text that they may want to share in discussion. Using the stems for response that are listed in the "sounds like" column of the chart in Figure 3.2, students are asked to write at least three to five responses to the passage.

We can model a tentative stance toward the text and invite student thinking by sharing some of our own responses to the text; ideally, we can avoid inferring and focus instead on things we notice, wonder about, and don't understand. This invites students to build understanding rather than rushing

Figure 3.3. Record of Class Discussion

Date: _____   Class: _____

Name	Ask a question (I wonder)	Share an observation (I notice)	Share an inference (I think)	Share a connection (I connect)	Share something confusing in the text (I don't understand)	Use the text to pursue an idea	Add to an idea (I'd like to add)	Interrupt	Hog discussion time	Put down someone's idea	Don't participate

to "answers." Often I see students rush to conclusions or interpretations of a text without lingering over and comprehending what's there. In order to help students develop better habits as readers, we therefore need to model what it sounds like to actively explore thinking through reading.

After the text has been read aloud and students have an opportunity to jot down their thinking, we can help them begin by sharing their responses. I also challenge students to keep their conversation going for 5 minutes without the teacher intervening. This is often a struggle for students, especially if they have been used to the teacher guiding all their responses and questions. I often use this opportunity to remind students that I'll be focusing on recording what they do in their conversation (using Figure 3.3) as a way to clearly separate my role from theirs. However, we can reserve the right to step in and facilitate as needed—as long as our purpose remains clearly to help students acquire and practice the skills of reading and discussion, not to take over the work of talking and thinking for them.

It is also critical that teachers refrain from making all the decisions about what is important in a text and what counts as "conversation worthy." Teaching students to build their understanding of the text through their own responses helps them understand reading as a process of meaning making. It also honors the diverse thinking of readers who may enter the same text in different ways and find different ideas worthy of thought and attention. For reading and discussion to enact socially just pedagogy, readers should have the right to their own ideas and the opportunity to voice them without being silenced by the teacher or by predetermined notions of what readings and ideas "count."

As students practice discussion with each other, we monitor and study their conversation using the chart in Figure 3.3. This provides us with ongoing assessment and a teaching tool: We can pause discussion at certain times to point out what moves students are making in their discussion or to ask them to try on a skill that they need to practice more explicitly. For example, we may notice that the group is doing a good job of taking turns and inviting participation, but that they shut down conversation by making statements about the text that attempt to answer questions in a perfunctory way without enabling the group to explore new thinking or grow their understanding of the bigger ideas in the text. After providing positive reinforcement for the discussion work they are doing well, we may ask the group to practice growing new questions from their original questions and testing out different ideas with evidence from the text.

If students struggle with these discussion moves, we can respond by focusing the next day's mini-lesson on ways to develop a line of inquiry. We might, for example, demonstrate how to develop new questions and responses off a given inquiry, using the following stems for thinking and discussion:

- This question leads me to wonder about . . . because . . .
- I wonder if . . .
- One possible interpretation might be . . .
- One place in the text that helps me think about this question is . . .

Once the routines of discussion are in place, I usually find that I no longer need the discussion chart to support students' independent discussion work. When this happens, the teacher's role can shift to become more of a recorder and coach. As students discuss their reading, we can keep a public record of their ideas by taking notes on an overhead or chart. This helps students keep track of the conversation and supports their listening and comprehension of one another's ideas. These notes do not need to be elaborate, just enough to summarize the topics and ideas the group is exploring.

We can also occasionally pause students' conversation to provide feedback on the discussion work they are approximating. These brief "time-outs" provide an opportunity to name what students are doing well in their discussion (e.g., "Notice how Jamal added to Selina's idea; this really helped to move your conversation forward"). It also creates an opportunity to show students the "data" reflected on the discussion chart and the public record and to assess themselves individually and plan for collective improvement. We can ask:

- What do you see yourself doing well in discussion right now? What more might you try?
- What does the group do well? What do you need to work on?
- Where are we getting stuck in our discussion? Let's talk about ways to solve the problems we're encountering.
- I'm noticing a lull in the conversation. Let's all stop and reflect on what's been said so far. Try writing down a new question or response before we resume our discussion. (Note: For this teaching move, it may be useful to have students revisit the public record we have created of their conversation; if there is no public written record, it helps to first summarize the ideas have been put forward.)

While it is important to coach students in their discussion as they try it, we also want to create opportunities for students to reflect on what they learned and need to work on at the end of the lesson. We can reserve the last 5 to 8 minutes of class to revisit the notes and chart from discussion (Figures 3.2 and 3.3), assess the group's progress in discussion, then ask students to write a written reflection before they leave. Some possible reflection questions include the following:

- What challenged you in discussion today? What do you think you need to work on to develop your reading and discussion skills?
- Look over the thoughts you had about the text before we began discussion. Now that you've had an opportunity to discuss others' ideas, what new thinking do you have about the text? How has your thinking changed?

Records of students' discussions, their written thinking on their texts, and their written reflections after discussion provide important insights into their reading and thinking processes. We can collect these samples of student work as a source of assessment to measure growth in students' discussion and thinking. Over time, we look for progress not only in students' discussions but also in the amount, nature, and quality of their thinking. We can also look for patterns of meaning in students' responses to determine what topics and ideas have relevance and implications for social justice. When studying student work, we can consider the following:

- What aspects of different texts do students tend to respond to?
- What connections do they tend to make to texts and what might this tell me about the funds of knowledge they bring to their reading and meaning making?
- What issues or meanings can I build on to pursue ideas about social justice?

RAISING THE LEVEL OF THINKING THROUGH STUDENT TALK

Once we get students talking, then what? Working from our assessment of students' initial efforts (see Figure 3.3), we can set goals for helping students learn to develop their reading and thinking while raising the level of conversation they have about texts. In order for classrooms to be characterized as cultures of thinking, students' talk needs to be *exploratory, accountable,* and *inclusive.* Working with these concepts helps us define next steps for instruction.

Exploratory talk refers to discourse that is characterized by the raising of questions and exploring of ideas by all members of the classroom community. Mercer, Wegerif, and Dawes's (1999) study of classroom instruction found that this mode of discourse created optimal conditions for learning. Mercer (2002) contrasts exploratory talk with classroom talk that focuses merely on procedures or tasks, rather than thinking:

Exploratory talk is that in which partners engage critically but constructively with each other's ideas. Relevant information is offered for joint consideration. Proposals may be challenged and counter-challenged, but if so reasons are given and alternatives are offered. Agreement is sought as a basis for joint progress. Knowledge is made publicly accountable and reasoning is visible in the talk. (p. 150)

Structuring discussion so that students learn how to ask questions—and are expected to do so—helps to support the development of exploratory talk. Beyond students' construction of their own questions and inquiries, though, they need support in learning how to improve their questions and collaboratively explore them through conversation in ways that acknowledge the voices and ideas of others.

The Institute for Learning at the University of Pittsburgh further defines good classroom talk as *accountable*. Students in classrooms with powerful conversations are accountable to the texts and ideas they are studying, to standards of reasoning, and to the learning community. This means we teach and expect students to do their best thinking through conversation and to continually assess their talk against the text itself and higher standards of reasoning that characterize good analysis and interpretation. Once we get students talking, then, there is often much more to teach.

Figure 3.4 shows one way to think about the progression of reading, writing, and thinking skills needed to construct a high-functioning literate community in the classroom. Each level is primarily descriptive and intended as a way of thinking about a progression of skills that students need in order to participate actively in a culture of thinking. While samples of lessons in this chapter focus on addressing particular levels through classroom instruction, this tool (chart) may also be used as a means to assess classrooms and determine a starting point for instruction: Which level(s) best describe the culture of a particular classroom that you teach? Where might you begin?

Alissa noted that, in her classroom, even though students diligently took notes on their reading and were willing to contribute to classroom discussions, the quality of their discussion faltered when they were unable to build on or extend one another's ideas in ways that focused their conversation on a train of thought. Rather than their pursuing one idea in depth, she saw her students throwing out different, unrelated ideas without knowing how to develop or extend any particular idea. She also noticed that they tended to get stuck when their own ideas were unclear. Using the scaffolding tool in Figure 3.4, Alissa and I assessed that students were generally working at Level 3 in their discussion. We therefore planned and co-taught a lesson to help the students in the class learn how to develop and clarify their collective thinking around one idea. The following transcript provides an example of instruction aimed at explicitly improving the level of students' discussion by pursuing a line of thinking. During the lesson, Alissa and I used multiple strategies that have been outlined thus far in this chapter. The transcript is intended as a model for considering how we can put these pedagogical strategies into practice.

In this sample lesson, students were trying to make meaning of literary motifs in the novel *Their Eyes Were Watching God*, by Zora Neale Hurston (1937). On the previous day, their discussion had faltered as students struggled to make sense of Hurston's use of literary motifs in connection with the main character, Janie, who struggles for freedom and dignity in her relationships with men, including her husband, Jody. As a novel by and about African American women and set in the South in the early 1930s, the text offers opportunities for students to explore and make sense of issues of gender, race, and power, as we see during the course of the following lesson.

A Sample Lesson in a Unit on Developing Better Discussions: Clarifying and Extending Our Thinking Through Discussion

Part 1: Establishing the Learning Goal and Purpose

Alissa: Last night I reflected in my notebook about your conversation yesterday, and I wanted to share my thinking with you. Given the criteria for discussion that we talked about yesterday (on the board), I saw some great things in your conversation. For example, you noticed a connection between some objects that Janie has, a handkerchief and an apron, and you started wondering more about the meaning of that in the text. Also, you invited participation. And what Scott said really pushed the conversation forward. Do you remember what Scott said?

Students: That the apron and handkerchief symbolize something.

Alissa: Yes. So then we pushed forward to see what we could do with this connection and what it might symbolize. You referred to the text a couple of times and began to explore a bigger idea about self-worth. I also noticed you struggled to develop your thinking in the conversation. Do you remember what happened?

Students: It was dead.

> Alissa constructs a meaningful purpose for the lesson, based on her observations of students' progress in discussion. Notice how she responds to students' efforts to identify specific things they did well in their conversation and to target a specific goal for the day.

Figure 3.4. Scaffolding Students' Thinking About Reading in Their Talk and Writing

	Level One	Level Two	Level Three	Level Four	Level Five
What Readers Do	Focus primarily on plot/summary Read text literally—do not go beyond the text Make literal level connections, but these do not lead the reader back to or beyond the text Talk about "facts" rather than ideas	Link responses to a specific part of the text Make basic inferences about a text (ex: informational inferences about plot or character) Focus on making meaning of parts of a text more than on the text as a whole	Elaborate on inferences by providing explanation or evidences for ideas about a text Build on ideas (their own or others') using standards of reasoning and textual evidence Build on ideas by linking several parts of a text together	Develop inferences about a whole text, analyzing how parts of the text fit together and build toward a larger idea (structure) Develop comprehensive, thematic interpretations of a text that are accountable to the text and standards of reasoning	Grow ideas in their independent reading and elaborate on those ideas in their written analyses of texts Lead and monitor their own discussions to build interpretations of texts
Goal	Students have their own thoughts to share in response to a text.	Students provide evidence for their thinking by being accountable to the text.	Students respond to, build on, and elaborate their ideas about a text in writing and discussion.	Students develop and refine big ideas about a text that synthesize details and parts of the text to create justifiable interpretations.	Students lead and monitor their own discussions, growing ideas on their own in group and independent reading.

Mini-lessons	How readers listen/attend in order to have something to say back to a text Marking texts with responses: *I think....* *I wonder...* *I notice...*	How readers use and refer to a text: *I think — because...* *An example of that is on page — ....* *What makes me say that is...* How to mark a text to develop thinking	How readers listen and share ideas in discussion: *Can you say more about —?* *I'd like to add to what — said...* *So what I hear you saying is...* How readers build on/revise an idea across a text How to link reading journal entries to revise or develop an idea	How to focus a discussion on a particular idea to build an interpretation Selecting a focus, sticking to it, and pursuing a line of inquiry as a group Reading for an idea across a whole text Synthesizing multiple journal entries about a text into a more elaborate interpretation	How to monitor and sustain a discussion independently How to keep talk focused and productive How to write about your ideas/interpretations of a text in a longer response to literature What a good literary analysis essay looks like
Methods	Teach discussion etiquette and ground rules for accountable talk Teach students how to say something during read-aloud/shared reading Name the moves students make in their talk and thinking Help students research their talk and make plans for improving	Demonstrate how to use the text and ask students to practice when saying something in partner or whole-class talk Guide whole-group discussion by bringing focus back to the text Name moves students make in their talk/thinking Help students research their talk and make plans for improving	Model building an idea (with a colleague/student) Students practice in whole-class discussion during read-aloud/shared reading Students practice in small groups with a shared text Name moves students make in their talk/thinking Help students research their talk and make plans for improving	Model building an idea across a novel (or longer text) using shared text Students jot down ideas/responses during or after reading; groups jot down ideas together Model how to make connections between different parts of the text Model how to talk/write about bigger ideas in a text over time	Students practice leading and monitoring their own talk in small groups; determine focus, agenda, and outcome(s) Teacher coaches groups in effective discussion and sophisticated analysis Groups research their talk and make plans for improving

Alissa: Yes. And I was thinking that one of the difficulties you faced was in really understanding the questions and ideas that were raised. So today we'll focus on clarifying our thinking throughout our discussion.

Part 2: Direct Instruction and Modeling of Discussion Skills

Laura: Today we'll work together to use two strategies to clarify our thinking: (1) asking questions of each other and (2) turning to the text. As we try these out, Mrs. Heikkila [Alissa] and I are going to see if you can try more of the discussion on your own. Learning to do discussion is hard work, and you have to practice. We want you to learn to make your literary conversation productive and to be able to do it independently.

So let's revisit. I understand you guys worked on this question yesterday. *[Taking notes on a piece of paper made visible by the document camera, Laura writes a student's question from the previous day: What am I learning more about Janie's journey though the author's use of the motif of Janie's hair?]* Whose question was that?

Student: Mine.

Laura: Thank you for the question. When I read your question . . . it struck me as a reader because I thought, "Oh, there are a lot of references to hair in here." I thought, What is that about? I know that authors deliberately bring things up. So there's something for us to figure out about the deeper meaning here. Now, the question "What am I learning more about Janie's journey through the author's motif about the hair?" had me a little confused initially. In order to clarify that for myself, I asked a bunch of smaller questions. Let's think for a minute: How can we take that question and break it down to even some smaller questions to help us focus so we can move our discussion forward? What questions can we think of in relation to this one that might help us clarify that a bit?

For example, I started wondering: When does the author talk about the hair? Is there some kind of situation in which she's usually bringing it up? And when I started to ask the smaller questions, it helped me clarify, "Oh, here's what I might think about." Talk to each other for a minute.

> The lesson begins with a student's question for shared inquiry. This is an important strategy for developing student ownership in the discussion. Notice that Laura scaffolds the reading work by modeling for students how to break down the question, then having them practice that thinking work through partner discussion.

What's a question that's related to our original one that might help us
clarify or direct our thinking further?
[Students in the class turn and talk with a partner for 2 minutes.]

Part 3: Guided Practice in Using Clarifying Questions

Laura: Let's collect some of these smaller, related questions that can help us
    clarify the idea we're pursuing. Ruiz is going to start us off. Tell us what
    your question is.
Ruiz: How is her hair a reflection of her environment?
Laura: Can you say more about that?
Ruiz: Like, she's in a town with a lot of Black people, and the Black people
    were under the White people. And Black people don't have long hair so
    she kind of stands out.
Laura: Okay—so how many people thought about
    that before? *[Two hands are raised.]* The fact that
    she has long hair and she's a Black woman, it
    makes her kind of stand out in a way.
Laura: *[On the overhead, Laura takes notes on what
    students are saying.]* Okay, so *town with a lot of
    Black women*—I'm just talking notes—*she has
    long hair, makes her stand out.* What's another
    question that might help us think about the
    idea of Janie's hair? I'm going to wait until I see
    a few more hands. . . . Okay, right back here.
Sasha: Okay, me and Jessica were thinking, in
    what other ways was Janie's hair symbolized?
    Through what other motifs?
Laura: Hmm. If I know some other ways I think
    her journey is symbolized maybe that will connect to the hair motif.
    Maybe that could help us figure out the hair. Okay—one more?
Terrance: Maybe how Janie's feeling emotionally with the hair or how is the
    hair described?
Laura: *[Writes down the idea]* How is the hair described? How does she feel about
    that? And why would that be important to notice?
John: Because if we are thinking that the hair represents something, it would
    probably be about Janie—how she's feeling?
Laura: Okay, one thing we can do as readers is that if we start to investigate
    some of these smaller questions, we may start to notice patterns. For
    example, let's say we start to look at a couple of different places in the
    text where they are talking about her hair, and we notice something that
    those passages have in common. Then we can say, "Hmmm, I'm noticing

> Taking notes on
> students' questions
> and ideas helps
> to build a culture
> of inquiry and
> gives all students
> equal access to the
> learning because
> they can visually
> keep track of the
> line of thinking in
> discussion. Students'
> ideas are valued as
> worthy of study.

this happens every time the author brings up hair. Maybe, the hair is supposed to mean . . . (something or other)." Does that make sense?

So you have all done a great job so far of asking smaller questions to help us clarify our thinking . . . now we want to go back and say, "How can we use the text to help us go deeper?" Let's take a look at two places in the text that mention Janie's hair. I want everyone to look at page 55. *[Laura places a photocopy of the text on the document camera.]* Let's see how we use the text to help us clarify our thinking. We've got all of these smaller questions to help

> Laura provides direct instruction in a reading strategy that will help students use their questions to explore and make meaning with the text.

us begin. *[Reads from the list of students' questions] What's going on in all these moments when the hair comes up? What's going on in the environment? What do we know about how's she connected to other Black women in the town? And what's going on with this hair?*

Part 4: Guided Practice in Using the Text to Extend Thinking and Discussion

Laura: I'm going to read this passage. After you hear it, I want you to discuss with your partner what you notice that connects to some of these questions that were raised. How is the hair described? How does she feel about it? What kinds of things are going on that have to do with Janie's hair that can help us figure out what it might mean? *[Laura reads a section of the novel from Chapter 6 (pp. 51–52).]*

> Laura reads the text aloud to help all students hear, understand, and work with the text. Students use their copy of the text to support comprehension and meaning making as they gather ideas with a partner. In this move, students are explicitly practicing the reading and discussion work in a focused, supported way.

> So this business of the head-rag irked her endlessly. But Jody [her husband] was set on it. Her hair was NOT going to show in the store. It didn't seem sensible at all. That was because Joe never told Janie how jealous he was. He never told her how often he had seen the other men figuratively wallowing in it as she went about things in the store. . . . She was there in the store for him to look at, not those others.

Laura: Talk to the person next to you now that you've heard this part of the text. Now what do we think the author might be trying to have us think about with this motif of the hair?

[Students turn and talk with a partner for 3 minutes. During this time, Laura and Alissa move around the room to listen in on students' partner discussions.]

Laura: Hank's going to start us off. Hank, what did you notice, what are you thinking about?

Hank: I said, like, her hair represents her body, and when Joe makes her tie up her hair he's basically controlling her and like owning her basically.

Laura: So it has something to do with Joe maybe controlling her? What do you mean by "controlling her"?

Hank: Kind of like making her hide herself—like she can't express herself.

Laura: Who can add to that?

Tehani: Joe's insecure. Like he knows he can be with her forever. But like he doesn't care 100% about how she feels.

Laura: I see lots of hands, which is great. I'm going to just point; I'm not going to say anything else and you guys are just going to keep the conversation going.

Taylor: Umm, everyone has their weak spots, and I guess he found her weak spot when he told her to put her hair up.

Jessica: It's kind of related to what Taylor said. You can tie in the whole age thing to this particular passage. It says that he's worried that other men are going to look at her and he doesn't want them to. And a lot of the time, people aren't going to look at *old* women.

> Because Laura and Alissa have listened carefully to students' reading and thinking in their partner discussions, they can now build on and scaffold students' thinking to help them analyze and interpret motifs in the text. Notice that students are doing the thinking work—not the teachers.

Laura: So let's look at one other passage. We've got a number of ideas here *[referring to the notes on students' ideas that she has been taking on the overhead]*. Here are some that I've heard so far: *Hair seems to be connected to age, control of men—Joe trying to control her, making her put her hair up. It may have something to do with ownership, and somebody said self-expression.* And these are all theories we are developing, but now we want to go back and mine the text one more time.

Let's take a look at another moment in the text and see what can we add to our thinking. Take a look at page 83. Janie is older now, and her husband, Joe, has died. *[Laura puts a section of the text under the document camera so that all students can see; students open their books to the same page.]* How does this scene connect back to some of the things we've noticed?

[Laura reads aloud from the end of Chapter 8 (p. 83).]

Then [Janie] thought about herself. Years ago, she had told her girl self to wait for her in the looking glass. It had been a long time since she had remembered. Perhaps she'd better look. She went over to the dresser and looked hard at her skin and features. The young girl was gone, but a handsome woman had taken her place. She tore off the kerchief from her head and let down her plentiful hair. The weight, the length, the glory was there. She took careful stock of herself, then combed her hair and tied it back up again. Then she starched and ironed her face, forming it into just what people wanted to see . . .

> Here Laura specifically scaffolds instruction to help students develop their ideas *across* the text. Deliberate and strategic choice and use of text helps students focus on the work of clarifying their ideas by working with the novel. Notice how issues of social justice and power are engaged through the reading work that students are doing.

Laura: So now, let's see if we can connect what happened here with what we saw in the other passage about hair. See any similarities? Any differences?

Pedro: So Joe starts off, "You need to tie your hair off," and as soon as he's gone like that first thing she did was she took off her handkerchief. I think that kind of symbolizes like she kind of felt some freedom and like she really valued her hair because everybody thought it was pretty. And so like, she let it down, and so she like it says, "Felt the length, the weight, and the glory," and I think that means that she was really happy about the fact that she could not be controlled by him anymore.

Laura: Can someone add to that? Ask a question or notice something else?

Tiffany: Um, I notice that in the beginning of the book it says that her mom was raped, by like a teacher, so throughout the whole story I'm kind of thinking that maybe the teacher was White and she got like the texture of her hair was kind of like . . . like mine—I don't know how to explain it—so I'm kind of thinking that she got her hair from the guy who raped her mom, and so that's why everyone kind of values it, 'cause it is different than most other people's so like they look at it differently. They kind of look at her like, ooooh, she's different from other people. It kind of makes her stand out.

> Notice how the issues of race that students bring forward are directly addressed and explored. Laura continues to connect students' responses to the overall purpose of clarifying ideas through discussion by honoring their ideas and pushing their investigation forward.

Laura: How many people remembered that? *[Several hands go up.]* What
　　page is that on?
Students: Page 19.
Laura: Do we know if the teacher was White? Do we have any evidence for
　　that? *[Students turn to page 19. A student reads a passage out loud to give
　　evidence for the idea that Janie's mother was raped by the teacher, who was
　　White.]*
Laura: Okay. He was White, so what about that? Why might that be
　　important for figuring out the motif of the hair?
Pedro: If her grandfather was White, that's some evidence that Janie has
　　some White in her.
Laura: Okay, so now we are saying *[writing notes projected on the document
　　camera]* the motif of the hair might connect to *age, control, ownership, self-
　　expression,* and possibly something about *race* and *Whiteness.* She's got
　　some Whiteness in her. Is it advantageous or disadvantageous for Janie?
　　How does that work? *[Students begin to talk at once.]* Okay, let's all do
　　some thinking about this, so turn and talk to your neighbor for a minute
　　and be ready to come back and say something about that.
[Students turn and talk excitedly with partners for 3 minutes.]
Laura: So what did you notice? Elena, you said something about beauty.
　　What did you say?
Elena: Like she's considered more beautiful than other girls because she has
　　that White in her. If she didn't her hair wouldn't
　　be as plentiful and beautiful and long. Black
　　people's hair is kind of short.
Tiffany: Like mine! *[Class laughs]*
Laura: So she has an advantage. She's considered
　　beautiful, right? What else about that?
Miguel: 'Cause beauty can bring her problems
　　kind of in a way. 'Cause she wants love, and she
　　attracts multiple guys 'cause of her hair. But then
　　all the guys want her because of her beauty. And
　　when a guy has her, he's more obsessed over
　　her than loves her. Like he wants her for him
　　because of her beauty.
Laura: So it attracts a lot of men but then they all
　　kind of control her—it comes back to this idea of
　　control?
Miguel: Yeah, because they don't want to share her
　　beauty.
Laura: Hmm . . . and if we go back to that question of whether it's an
　　advantage or disadvantage for her to have this hair, where do we

> Here Laura builds
> on the ideas of
> one student, Elena,
> whose voice has
> not yet been heard
> in whole-group
> discussion. Elena, a
> Mexican American
> student, brings the
> issue of Whiteness
> and privilege to the
> foreground, enabling
> the rest of the class
> to consider the role
> of race in the text.

see other places where she gets one or the other; does she get any other advantages or disadvantages?

Sarah: Disadvantage because her husband treats her like a trophy.

John: I think that it could be an advantage or disadvantage; sometimes she wants it and uses it to her advantage because on page 27, right when she first met Joe, she let her hair down on purpose. And she knew that if she flaunted her hair like that she would get the attention from him.

> Notice how Laura raises new questions in response to Elena's observation. This allows students to elaborate on the ideas of control and power as an issue of social justice.

Laura: Okay, so it's something she can use for power so the hair might be connected in some way to her having at least some kind of power. Okay . . . anything else?

Omar: Building on what John said, when Janie runs off with Tea Cake [another man], Mrs. Turner sees Janie as kind of above her—'cause she has the really nice hair and a lighter complexion.

Laura: Okay, so this goes back to that question about Whiteness. What are you saying about that exactly?

Omar: Mrs. Turner doesn't really like any other Black people and she kind of views herself as being above Black people, 'cause she has sharp features and a slightly pointed nose and is proud. And then Janie comes through and she has really long hair and a lighter complexion, and Mrs. Turner envies that. Mrs. Turner holds herself above Black people and holds Janie above herself.

> Because the goal is for students to learn new habits and ways of discussing their ideas—not just with this novel but with any text—it is critical that they understand and reflect on how those strategies were applied and how this supported their development as better readers and discussants.

Laura: So it seems significant that she has a mixed-race background. In some ways, the things people associate with her being White seem to allow her to have some privileges. I mean, she's the mayor's wife, right? But what does Joe do to her the whole time they are in their marriage?

John: Tries to control her.

Laura: He tries to control her, but he also puts her on a pedestal, right? And at the same time, she doesn't have privileges in a certain sense because she is a woman. So in the time we have left, I want you to go back to our question. Now that we've worked on clarifying and extending our thinking by asking questions and using the text, what do you think that the motif of Janie's hair represents in the text? Use the notes from our discussion to help you write your response.

[During the last 5 minutes of class, all students thoughtfully write in their notebooks.]

Reflecting on the Lesson: Unpacking Socially Just Teaching in Action

This class was taught during a shortened, 30-minute period in a class of 25 students. During that time, every student actively, purposefully engaged in reading, writing, and thinking together. This did not happen by accident, or through the magical class combination of "good kids." It happened through purposeful, strategic instruction focused on developing students' thinking through discourse.

The content of the lesson—the themes of racial injustice and gender inequity that permeated students' discussion—helped students to explore important concepts of social justice through their reading and discussion of the text. And because the lesson targeted students' discussion work, they were able to engage in Level 4 work (see Figure 3.4) through purposeful guided practice. In later days, Alissa would give students opportunities to practice Level 4 work through partner and small-group discussions of the text, thus gradually releasing them to greater levels of independence and ownership in their reading, thinking, and discussion.

Interviewed at the end of the year about the ways in which Alissa's instruction had helped him, one student, Chino, explained, "This class is tough, but it has helped a lot by giving me a lot of strategies for getting you interested in what you are doing. I'm learning how to come up with my own original ideas . . . and I'm going to use this forever." By helping all students learn to talk and think with greater agency and interdependence, we work toward ensuring that they can exercise the right to their own ideas—and make them grow.

CHAPTER FOUR

Teaching for Ownership and Independence

Helping Students Develop Purpose for Their Learning

Just give me the words so I can use them how I want.

—Derek, 9th-grader

DEREK EXPRESSED THE PRECEDING sentiment to me when, as a researcher, I interviewed him about his work in language arts class at a Detroit-area high school. For Derek, the point of learning was to develop a language he could use for his own powerful purposes. He was a student who engaged for the most part compliantly with his work in school, and yet his statement also reflects a frustration toward the need for purpose and agency in his own learning and a belief that the role of the teacher is to just "give the words."

In recent years, I've heard growing concern from teachers who care deeply about their students' learning, but who share similar observations of how young people are engaging (or not) in school, and how purpose affects their learning. A lack of purpose and ownership might take various forms:

- *Students faking their learning and reading.* Strong and weak readers alike at times go through the motions of reading. This can look like students skimming a text rather than reading closely, texting beneath their desk, or outright avoidance, at all costs, of engaging with reading work.
- *Students engaging passively in classroom reading and learning.* At times this looks like students with their heads down and disconnected from the classroom; at other times, it is expressed in students' task-driven approach to classroom work such that they do not bring their own thoughts, ideas, or cares to the learning. At times, these students finish tasks without being able to discuss or reflect on what they learned or why they learned it.

These problems can occur even when the curriculum focuses on content deemed to be culturally relevant for students. The issue, I think, lies partly in who decides what is purposeful for whom.

Teaching is fundamentally built on the relationship between the teacher, the student(s), and the work of learning; this is also a relationship of power and therefore a focus for the development of socially just teaching practice. Ideally, students are empowered to seek new learning and pursue knowledge and understanding that they feel will better their lives in some way. Yet learning is an act of submission; we seek knowledge for a reason, pursue that which we do not (yet) know, and rely on texts and others to teach us. Where the role of the learner in this relationship is one that is characterized by reception and submission, without the power to construct a purpose or relevant personal goals for learning, students may not learn to develop agency in their own lives as learners. Creating, through powerful teaching, the conditions for developing purposeful reading and learning is therefore an important part of the work of socially just teaching.

INDEPENDENCE AND OWNERSHIP
AS MATTERS OF SOCIAL JUSTICE

Several years ago, I attended an art exhibit entitled *Edward Hopper's Women* at the Seattle Art Museum. The exhibit featured paintings by the American artist that focused on his portrayal of women in the 1920s and 1930s, reflecting the social transformation that was occurring at that time with the entrance of women into the urban working world. The paintings haunted and disturbed me. The women in these images looked unhappy and lonely, as though they didn't belong in the worlds they so newly inhabited. As a working mother, I found myself wondering how the women themselves thought about their own social choices and positions, and how they experienced the demands of family and society while seeking their own fulfillment outside of the home. The meanings in art resonated with a personal inquiry I have pursued for a long time in my own intellectual and reading life: How do women navigate the demands and constraints of gender expectations while seeking a fulfilled life? How do they overcome adversity and gender oppression to live in an empowering way?

When I reflected on my own reading life, I realized that many of the texts I often read were somehow connected to my inquiry and helped me make sense of it in some way. I had read Leo Tolstoy's *Anna Karenina*, Jane Austen's *Mansfield Park,* and Zora Neale Hurston's *Their Eyes Were Watching God* to consider how women chose their relationships and how these were shaped by class and gender. I had read *Beloved*, by Toni Morrison, and *The Good Mother*, by Sue Miller, to make sense of how social ideas and expectations of women as mothers, as well as the injustices they faced in their lives, shaped women's opportunities and choices. All along, I pursued my own questions and sought answers through my reading that could help me make sense of my own life and what it means for me to be a woman in a society in which so much depends, often subtly, upon gender and power.

When I consider my own reading life in this way, the work of reading— and of literary analysis—is deeply personal, political, and purposeful. And I want this kind of reading life for students.

In a socially just classroom, learners are empowered to develop meaningful purposes for their own learning, and students' individual and collective learning occur in a mutually dependent and beneficial relationship. In Alissa Niemi Heikkila's 11th-grade classroom, for example, students developed and pursued their own personal inquiries to guide their reading and literary analyses. The following list reflects some of the questions that defined their purposes for learning:

- How does questioning oneself affect one's journey in life? (Indigo)
- What are the variables that influence a person's pursuit of purpose in life? (Chino)
- Why do we allow fear to control our lives? (Paloma)
- Are all men/women really created equal? (Jim)
- What do people base respect on? Why do people decide to respect some people and not others? (Erica)
- How do cultural backgrounds affect friendship? (Kiyomi)

While the role of social justice curriculum that teachers bring *to* students is important for developing social awareness and critical literacy, the work of personal inquiry empowers students to develop the curriculum *with* teachers. By developing personal inquiries, students consider what issues matter in their own lives and how these pertain to the work of building a more socially just world. The students in Alissa's class used their questions to develop ideas through small-group reading of several works of literature, including *The Sound of Waves*, by Yukio Mishima, and *A Doll's House*, by Henrik Ibsen. Their questions not only reflected personal meaning but also laid the groundwork for developing a shared focus on how inequities and injustices play out in people's lives. Chino's inquiry, for example, was in part an attempt to make sense of his own identity as an African American male and to understand what factors might shape his opportunities and life chances. Through personal inquiry, students learned to develop meaningful questions and pursue them through their reading as a means to develop socially significant interpretations of text. As members of a learning community, students shared and explored personally and socially relevant meanings in their reading lives.

In order to develop powerful instruction for every student, students need agency in their own learning work. Empowered learners can talk about what they are learning, how they are making choices and exercising agency in that learning, and why it all matters in the first place.

Rex and Schiller (2009) note that power is always exchanged through the social interaction that occurs in the classroom, and that the teacher's goal should be one of developing and maintaining inter/relationships while building new knowledge as a community. They propose that teachers "circulate" power through the classroom as a means to foster students' individual agency while constructing a democratic learning community that fosters shared understanding through collaboration. Alissa's approach to reading as personal inquiry work exemplifies one way to circulate power to students by giving them a bigger stake in their own reading process.

Research has shown that engagement in reading is critical not only for students' comprehension but also for their literate development, as students read most powerfully and successfully when they are engaged and purposeful in their interactions with texts (Cummins, 2007; Ruddell & Speaker, 1985). Even more important, engaged, purposeful reading can even help to mitigate inequities in students' reading achievement that are often sustained through social inequalities—offering a powerful argument for the importance of addressing reading through socially just teaching practice (Cummins, 2007).

For high school students, reading work often requires that they engage with complex texts chosen by the teacher or dictated by curricular guidelines. For struggling and proficient readers (and their teachers), this can create further challenges for engagement. Yet readers will persevere and comprehend material that is considerably harder than material at their reading level if they have high interest in the content (Shnayer & Robinson, 1969); furthermore, students' motivation, attitude, and interests strongly influence their ability to pay attention to the text, to comprehend, and to think deeply about the content (Belloni & Jongsma, 1978). The more that students' reading is aligned to their own goals and purposes, the more they will persist in their thinking with and about the text—even when that text is challenging or at the reader's frustration level.

At issue in the teaching of reading, then, is the shift toward conceptualizing and enacting reading as a process of inquiry that allows students' questions to inform curriculum that is co-constructed by teacher and students. Where many students' conception of reading is transmissive, with texts serving as an end, we seek to create conditions for reading as exploration, where texts serve as a beginning point in an ongoing process of discovery and thinking in ways that matter to students' lives and communities.

Because purpose drives the reading process and the motivation for learning (Guthrie, 2004), I developed, and Alissa implemented, a personal inquiry unit of study in order tackle the problem of ownership head on. In the next section, I will outline the reading inquiry approach as one method for directly instructing and coaching students in how to develop purpose and ownership in their reading. Along the way, I will illustrate what this work looked like in the classroom with Alissa's students.

AN OVERVIEW OF A UNIT IN READING
AS PERSONAL INQUIRY

A unit on personal inquiry, conceived as a social justice project, develops explicit literacy skills for students' reading, writing, and thinking. The work of the unit creates a foundation for helping students develop an inquiry stance and the habits of active inquirers. An overview of the student outcomes is noted in Figure 4.1.

Personal inquiry work aims to help students understand and develop habits for learning that will drive and sustain their future learning. We want students to know *how* to develop their curiosities and skills in ways that empower them to have a stake in their own learning and thinking.

The unit outlined here may be used in various ways. For Alissa and her students, their curriculum was narrowly defined by the need to teach district-directed texts. She used the approach to help students create a purpose for reading the novels *Sound of Waves*, by Yukio Mishima, and *Their Eyes Were Watching God*, by Zora Neale Hurston. While each of these novels offers rich possibilities for exploring themes of oppression, their function as mandated texts limited possibilities for students to develop ownership through their choice of text. Alissa chose, therefore, to use the reading inquiry unit to help students learn ways to develop purposes for exploring the texts on their own terms.

A personal inquiry unit may also be organized to provide greater choices with regard to texts and ways of reading. In one 7th-grade class, I worked with the teacher to help students develop their own inquiries. We then gathered all of the students' questions and grouped students according to similar interests that were reflected in their inquiries. One group, for example, we loosely named "Overcoming Adversity" because students' questions reflected the struggles they faced in their lives as they tried to make sense of death, illness, and family hardship. Seeing students' interests put so vividly, the teacher and I went to the library to gather as many books as possible to match them. When students arrived in class the next day, they were grouped at tables with other readers of like inquiries and a pile of books to inspect for their relevance to the readers. Students learned how to assess books for their readability and

Figure 4.1. Student Literacy Outcomes for a Unit on Personal Inquiry

As Thinkers, Students Will ...	As Readers, Students Will ...	As Writers, Students Will ...
Develop a guiding question that reflects a meaningful and personal purpose for learning	Develop a purposeful plan for reading, built around the pursuit of a personally and socially significant question	Construct and revise questions and subquestions to clarify thinking
Develop subquestions that reflect an understanding of what one needs to learn in order to make sense of the larger inquiry	Use their question to engage with text, to create subquestions, and develop a line of thinking that reflects new learning and understanding	Construct ongoing, written responses to text that extend the inquiry through grounded examination and reflection on text
Consider one's prior knowledge about the question in light of new ideas and information, continually reflecting on and revising one's question(s)	Make connections between their question, their text(s), and their lives and communities	Develop idea(s) in response to the inquiry over time by comparing previous written responses, elaborating on a concept and how it is embodied in text, and revising the expression of an idea in writing
Engage in methodological believing and doubting about one's developing understanding of text to consider the following: What fits with my current thinking/ understanding? What doesn't fit? What complicates my thinking and how can I refine my understanding?	Read to develop and refine their thinking in response to the inquiry in order to develop an informed thesis that addresses the question	Construct and revise a thesis that addresses the original inquiry Synthesize the results of inquiry in a comprehensive written response (essay or longer formal response) that presents and explains ideas to a reader and establishes purpose

relevance and were asked to develop a reading plan with at least three books related to their inquiry. Many students who had previously been disengaged in their reading were suddenly animated, swapping and discussing books with members of their newfound groups and sharing their questions and stories with one another. At the end of the class period, students turned in a draft of their Reading Plan, in which they created a list of books they wanted to read for their inquiry, a reflection on what they hoped to learn and why, and the names of students at their table group with whom they would work well. Ultimately, then, students developed long-term plans for their reading projects, thereby increasing their chances of ongoing engagement in learning.

Regardless of the specific organization, a personal inquiry approach focuses on the thinking work of reading as an inquiry process. The process has three phases, as outlined in Figure 4.2.

Figure 4.2. Phases of Instruction in a Unit on Personal Inquiry

What Mini-Lessons Focus On	What Students Are Doing as Independent Readers
Phase 1: Before Reading	
How to develop an inquiry and purpose for reading	Developing an inquiry (and subquestions)
How to select texts according to your purpose (inquiry)	Previewing texts in order to make purposeful selections
What an inquiry-based reading process looks like	Determining reading partnerships or groups, based on shared interests
	Reflecting in writing on why their inquiry matters to them
Phase 2: During Reading	
How to use your inquiry to develop a line of thinking as you read	Marking their thinking on the text (with adhesive notes) to develop connections to their inquiry
Developing theories in response to your inquiry (e.g., Based on my reading, a possible response to my inquiry is . . .)	Writing long notebook entries off of key responses and passages from the text
	Discussing key questions and passages in order to develop theories with partners, small groups, or the whole class
Phase 3: After Reading	
Using the notebook to synthesize your ideas across the whole text	Rereading adhesive notes, notebook entries, and key passages to develop a thesis about the text, based on their inquiry
Using evidence from the text to develop your theory into a thesis	Collecting and writing off passages from the text that help them develop their thesis
Developing a longer piece of writing that explores and elaborates on your thesis, using material developed through adhesive notes and notebook entries	Synthesizing multiple notebook responses into a finished piece of writing

Phase 1: Developing the Inquiry Before Reading

The first phase of the unit offers students the opportunity to see a model of what personal inquiry can look like in an authentic reading life. When introducing personal inquiry to Alissa's students, for example, I shared the story of my inquiry on women's roles and told the story of how my question shaped my reading life. I shared slides of Hopper's artwork with students, along with a stack of books that I had read—or was going to read. I narrated the story of my inquiry and how my reading of each text helped me to deepen my understanding of my question, to find answers, and to develop new and related questions that sustained my thinking and engagement with the inquiry. When Alissa launched the unit with her other classes, she modeled her own personal inquiry as well.

As the inquiry and reading process is modeled, we can ask students to notice *how* we developed a purpose for our reading. This step helps students to see real purposes for reading and name strategies they can then use to develop their own inquiries. Students' observations can then be charted and the chart used to support students' independent work as they develop their own inquiries during independent reading time. A sample chart developed with Alissa's students is shown in Figure 4.3.

The process of developing an inquiry and reading plan took several days. To get students started, we gave them several strategies for reflection:

Figure 4.3. Classroom Strategy Chart Developed in Response to a Model of Personal Inquiry

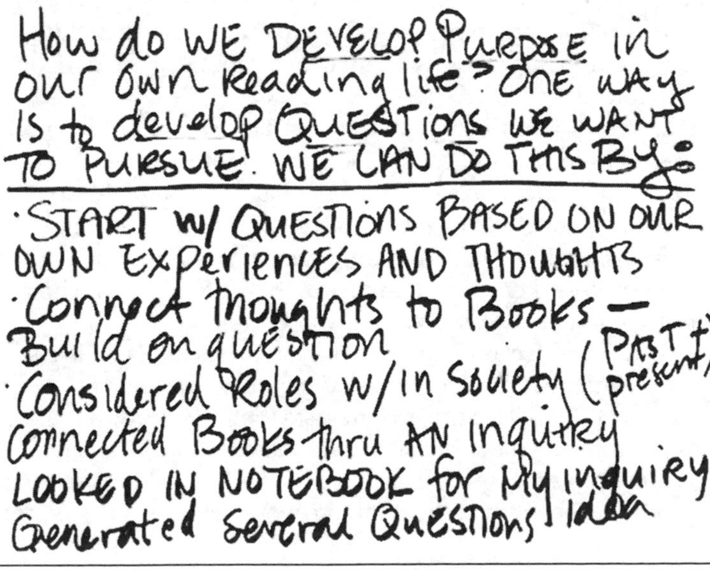

How do WE DEVELOP Purpose in our own Reading life? One way is to develop Questions we want to pursue. WE CAN DO This BY:
- START w/ Questions BASED ON OUR OWN Experiences AND Thoughts
- Connect thoughts to Books —
Build on question
- Considered Roles w/in Society (Past/present)
Connected Books thru AN inquiry
LOOKED IN NOTEBOOK for My inquiry
Generated Several Questions! idea

- Make a list of texts you've read (include fiction, nonfiction, and various text types, including songs) that have been important to you. This may be a recent list or a list that spans a period of time.

—OR—

- Develop a list of your burning questions: What do you wonder about that you really want an answer to . . . and why do these questions matter?
- Look for patterns or themes: What do any of your reading obsessions or burning questions have in common? How might some of your texts or questions be connected to a larger inquiry?

As students developed their inquiries, Alissa strategically built community by having them share their inquiries and tell the story of where their question(s) came from. Students' questions were recorded on a class chart that captured each student's inquiry and class suggestions for how the student could pursue his or her question. Such a practice fosters interdependence and helps to construct the shared story of "who we are as learners and people in this class." Having students post and share their questions also helps them to refine their thinking and clarify the questions themselves, which (ideally) are revised over time to better reflect the thinker's focus and intention. In the following recollection, Alissa describes what she noticed about students' reading and how she responded in strategic ways to develop a supportive community for exploring ideas that had power and purpose in students' lives.

As students began to read with their personal inquires I noticed they were doing a great job of finding places in the text that made them think about their inquiry, but I also noticed student conversations seemed robotic and sometimes forced.

I realized that I was asking them to read in a way that was new and that I needed to model and coach them in what it meant to have a personal inquiry and how that's different than just reading with a question in mind. Because I was asking students to explore and investigate text on personal levels, and I realized the importance of community support in the reading process, I chose to do most of the scaffolding in whole-class shares rather than mini-lessons.

I began to start off class share sessions by suggesting outside resources to particular students: "Carina, I know your inquiry is around appearances. I was watching this TED lecture on feminism that I think you should check out. Here, I wrote down the website. I really liked how the presenter compared past and present views on women's roles." I could tell that Carina was excited that I spent the time thinking about her outside of school and this helped her find relevance in her inquiry. I would then ask the class, "Has anyone else read or seen something that would help Carina think about her inquiry?"

Students would share all sorts of responses, from movies they'd seen, anecdotes of family members struggling with their identity, books or articles they'd read, and lessons they'd learned. These types of shares became routine. As we started getting comfortable sharing our inquiries, students began to facilitate the shares and voluntarily brought in resources and suggestions for one another.

As the ideas started to pile up, we created a personal inquiry chart where students would write their suggestions on adhesive notes and stick them on the chart. The energy in the classroom shifted—students would come to class early to post a suggestion and to see if someone had an idea for their inquiry. It added an element of authenticity and excitement around the reading process.

The class shares helped students see their purpose for reading beyond just the pages of the book in front of them. The biggest class shift, however, came from Carina's inquiry share. Periodically, a student would facilitate a class share around an inquiry, oftentimes with my coaching. Most often, this would include analyzing a particular passage and helping the facilitator break down his or her inquiry. It was Carina's turn and her share looked and sounded different.

Carina began by telling the class how she came up with her personal inquiry: "I was thinking about all the movies I watch and the books I love and they all have women that are insecure; they are worried about how they look and all they want is a boyfriend or husband. I began to think about myself and how I'm always worried about being pretty and boys liking me." Then Carina began to break down and cry. The class was speechless. Students began to look at me for what to do next.

Maddy was first to speak up, saying, "Carina, you are so naturally pretty and smart." Students then began to follow with complimentary comments that eventually turned into questions such as "Why do you think you feel insecure?" and "What are some times that you feel most confident?" These reflective questions guided a meaningful conversation that helped all students see the relevance in what and how they are reading. Because Carina took a risk, students started to open up and truly care about each other and their inquiries. (Alissa, Interview)

This phase of the study also provides the teacher with an opportunity to mine students' questions and stories for themes related to social justice that can be highlighted and focused on through shared reading. In Alissa's class, for example, many of students' questions focused on how individuals make choices in their lives and how they navigate their social world. As sites for exploring ideas of social justice, the teacher might choose texts for whole-class reading that allow students to consider their personal inquiry alongside the following whole-class inquiry: How do we best reconcile the needs and interests of individuals in creating communities that are "just"? Building the class focus in this way therefore honors the purposes and funds of knowledge (Moll, 1992) students bring to the classroom while creating opportunities for the teacher to guide the group's thinking to inquiries that can help them ex-plore concepts pertaining explicitly to social justice.

Phase 2: Using One's Inquiry to Guide Reading Work

Once students have developed their inquiries, the second phase of study focuses on how to use one's inquiry to deepen reading and thinking. This is where the most important reading work takes place. Because the study focuses on helping students become more engaged, purposeful, and proficient in their reading, mini-lessons provide opportunities for direct instruction, modeling, and guided practice with text before students pursue the thinking work of their inquiries independently. We want to see students use their questions to mine the text, reflect on what they are learning, and revisit their inquiry with new eyes.

Alissa found that as her students began reading with their inquiries, their thinking began to falter and they weren't applying their questions to the text; in other words, although they had established a purpose for their reading and learning, they left their question behind once they began reading and focused instead on merely tracking the plot—a habit she had hoped to move them beyond. To help students develop a line of thinking with their text and inquiry, she developed some of the mini-lessons in Figure 4.4 to help students better understand the reading work they were asked to undertake.

Figure 4.4. Mini-lessons for Reading with a Personal Inquiry in Phase 2

- Why should we read with a personal inquiry, and how will it help us better make meaning of text?
- How do I break down my inquiry to read for subtleties/subquestions and why is that important?
- How do I closely analyze the text with my inquiry lens?
- How do I shift/change my inquiry?
- How can I use my adhesive notes and notebook entries to support my reading process?
- How do I know what passages to focus on and how do I analyze passages to develop sophisticated theories and questions?
- How do I transition from reading with an inquiry lens (a question) to developing a seed idea for writing?

For each lesson, Alissa used a shared text to model and engage students in practicing the thinking work involved with their inquiry. Because her students were reading one of several texts during the study, she drew short passages from those texts to demonstrate the reading work in which she wanted all students to engage (regardless of which text they read). In classrooms organized around a wider array of text choices, the teacher might choose other short text excerpts or a longer class text from which each lesson would draw. What is essential, however, is to scaffold instruction to help students engage in independent reading work so that the teacher can see and build upon whatever students are able to do on their own with the text.

In the following lesson example, Alissa used the gradual release framework (Pearson & Gallagher, 1983) to teach a lesson on *how* to use one's inquiry while reading. Using this approach, she first demonstrated and provided guided practice in the reading process before asking students to try on the work independently. Alissa developed the lesson after seeing that students struggled to apply their questions to their meaning-making process with the texts they were reading. Here she used a student's inquiry as a basis for the lesson by having the whole class practice using the student's question while reading the same text.

The lesson offers an example of socially just teaching practice in several ways. First, Chino, whose inquiry is used as an example in the lesson, was a student who had struggled in Alissa's class and had considered dropping out. Her choice to work with Chino's inquiry helped to validate his interests and efforts, as well as the quality of his inquiry question. Second, the lesson uses the gradual release model to ensure that all students get support and practice for the thinking work they are asked to take on. Notice how Alissa expects *every* student to try on the reading work, tailors her instruction to students' responses and abilities as readers, and builds upon their contributions. Notice, too, where students' meaning making with the text creates possibilities for a deeper understanding of issues pertaining to social justice.

Transcript of a Lesson on Personal Inquiry: How to Use Your Inquiry to Deepen Your Reading and Thinking

Part I: Alissa Introduces the Purpose of the Lesson

Alissa: So in looking at the notes you've done on your inquiries, I'm really impressed with how you all are taking your inquiries and looking outside of school. I read how you watched a movie and that made you think about your inquiry; I heard Andrew talk about how a conversation on the phone made him think about his inquiry. So I'm noticing that's a strength of yours as a class.

One thing that I'm also noticing is that you're not doing as well when it comes to *reading* for your inquiry. That's where the difficulty lies. For today, let's get some more practice in how we read for our inquiry, and in doing so, how do we narrow it down? What do we focus on when we read?

We're going to work with Chino's inquiry today. We're going to support Chino and give Chino a little love. I also noticed that, Kelsey, your inquiry is very similar to Chino's, just worded a little bit differently—I don't know if you knew that. So Chino is going to talk about his inquiry, but you can chime in if you like.

> Notice that the purpose of the lesson comes from Alissa's assessment of—and response to—students' work. She creates relevance by helping students understand where they need to grow as readers and cultivates interdependence by using Chino's work and having the class practice with his inquiry.

Part 2: Using a Student Model to Develop and Illustrate the Lesson

Alissa: So, Chino, your inquiry is, *What are the variables that affect a person's pursuit of purpose in life?* Talk to us a little bit about why this is important to you and how you came to this.

Chino: Okay, so first I had this kind of reality-type idea like, *What is reality?*, or, *What develops someone's reality?* And I thought about books and movies I like, and certain books like *Brave New World* . . . *[Chino reaches for the books he brought to share]* A lot of them have to do with like someone's point of view of something, or like one reality to another. . . . So, *Harry Potter*, for instance, you have the magical world then you have the Muggles or humans, so a lot of them kind of had to do with one reality and another reality. So within that idea, I thought about roles in life and purpose in the world. So how, I guess, within one's reality, how they come across their purpose in life and what they want to do. So certain questions were, like, *How do you know your purpose in life or what's possible? What are the variables that affect an individual's purpose in life?* And *How do relationships affect your roles?* And I had this idea of silent agreements, because I went to the leadership conference, and Eric's mom talked to us about the idea of silent agreements. That's, for example, like in a relationship you expect the guy to work and the woman to stay home. And I found it interesting that—that's how things are now. . . . And that led

> Notice how Chino's question develops from many different areas of his life and how he has acquired the agency to talk about his own thoughts and purposes.

me to make smaller questions, which led me to, What are the factors that influence a person's pursuit of purpose in life?

Alissa: Okay, that's great.

[Alissa now puts up on the overhead a copy of a passage from The Sound of Waves, by Yukio Mishima. On the left side of the photocopy there is blank space in which she has written Chino's question, along with the heading "Ways We Can Read for This Inquiry."]

Part 3: Students Practice Focusing the Inquiry and Setting a Purpose for Reading

Alissa: So we're going to look at Chino's inquiry and think about how we can we break this down as readers and what can we focus on. Take a second, and on the left-hand side here, list all of the ways that as readers we can focus on Chino's question.

[All students work silently to list things to focus on while reading that might help one to explore Chino's question.]

Alissa: Once you've exhausted your brain power, turn and talk to each other: What are all the ways we can read for this question?

[At Alissa's signal, students turn and talk to one another about their ideas. The following conversation takes place among three students, one of whom is Chino.]

Kyle: I said one way was to focus on the authorial intent behind a character's pursuit of purpose. And how the pursuit affects other characters, or the character development.

Chino: Mine is kind of the same as what you said, but also how your purposes can shift or change over time. Like how it changed before or after characters meet. I put stereotypes, too. I feel like stereotypes are a big thing, because certain people may feel like they can't do things because of stereotypes.

> Notice how Alissa turns over the thinking work to students, giving time for diverse ideas and possibilities to develop. In this conversation, Chino raises the issue of stereotypes as an obstacle to one's aspirations.

Kyle: I think like inspiration, too. Like in Pursuit of Happyness, he was inspired to do things for his son. So maybe the inspiration for what a person is pursuing is important, too.

[Alissa draws the class back together, ending students' conversations.]

Alissa: So as readers, what are some ways we can best investigate Chino's question?

Carina: I think there are different things that might influence it, like family and relationships. Different cultures or different generations. Like for example, if you wanted to go to a certain college, but your parents want you to go to a different one; or if you want to marry someone of a different culture [and they have a different choice]. That may sway how you make your decisions.

Alissa: So you're looking at the role that family plays in influencing the pursuit of purpose.

[Alissa writes up an example on the overhead: family/relationships/cultures; how they influence the decision.]

Carina: Right.

As students continued to share their ideas, Alissa captured and wrote them up on the overhead as a means to help students understand different ways to focus their reading and attention with the text. This strategy helped to promote students' identities as learners and thinkers and gave them visual access to the ideas forwarded in discussion. Figure 4.5 captures what students saw on the overhead during the lesson.

Part 4: Alissa Provides Guided Reading Practice with the Text

Alissa: So as we're reading, we're focusing on these different things . . . I'm going to read aloud, and I'd like you to think about these different ways of reading and how can they help us think about this question of a person's pursuit of purpose.

[Alissa reads the first paragraph of the text aloud as students follow along on their copy.]

Figure 4.5. Co-Constructed Notes from Personal Inquiry Reading Lesson

Chino's Question:

What are the variables that affect an individual's pursuit of purpose in life?

Using the preceding inquiry question to guide our reading, what could we focus on to deepen our reading and thinking with the text?

What We Can Focus on as a Reader

- family/relationships/culture (how they influence decisions)
- what motivates the character?
- why is the motivation important?
- what does the character have or want?
- what makes the character happy?
- stereotypes—what the character can and can't do
- identify the purpose (what character thinks his/her purpose is)

Alissa: So right away, some things that I'm noticing are that Shinji is a fisherman, right? And it's taking him an *hour* just to get to his job. So I'm wondering now, how does his isolation on the island, and maybe his occupation, perhaps hinder his pursuit of purpose? [*Alissa writes on the text: How does isolation or occupation affect his purpose?*] Is there anything else that stands out to you in this first chunk? Maria?

Maria: I noticed it said, "Boarded his master's boat as usual." This made me wonder if it's something he really *enjoys* doing. It sounds like it's just routine, like it's something he doesn't want to be doing but he has to do.

Alissa: And it's not *his* boat, is it?

Maria: Right.

[*As students continue to share ideas, Alissa takes notes on the text to reflect connections they are making to Chino's inquiry and how this is developing their line of thinking. At the end of the lesson, Alissa asks students to reflect on what they are noticing about how to read for an inquiry.*]

> Notice how students begin to see potential topics for social justice. Maria's observations point to issues of social roles and relationships of power that may affect the character's opportunities as a member of a subordinated social group.

As students named the reading moves they made during the lesson, Alissa charted the strategies and steps of the reading process they used to make meaning. The chart then supported students' independent reading work with their own text as the next step in their learning process.

Alissa's lesson demonstrates how the work of engaging students in personal inquiry not only helps students develop purpose but also provides explicit instruction and support for reading to help students gain access to texts and ideas at higher levels. Rather than being told "the themes" or social justice content of a work of literature or being asked to answer the teacher's questions, students gain the knowledge and power to develop their own ideas and to read powerfully and critically for those ideas. Alissa's use of students' questions and work to drive the learning reflects a deep commitment to making learning culturally and personally relevant and empowering to students themselves.

It would be easy, however, to focus on how the form of teaching in this example reflects ideals of socially just teaching practice without looking carefully at the content of instruction and its implications for social justice. After all, students are reading and discussing a text that, while its choice reflects an attention to multicultural literature (as the work of a Japanese author), it may not be considered political enough to receive attention as a choice for social justice curriculum. Notice, however, that Alissa's decision to focus on Chino's inquiry directs the students' attention to how social factors shape individuals' opportunities. Students' questions and observations about the text pinpoint rich material for developing a deeper understanding of how class and social location can inscribe the lives and purposes of individuals and how one's goals in life can be hindered when at odds with social expectations. As high school students are just beginning to make sense of the wider social world, they need opportunities to develop their understanding of how injustice "works" and the many social mechanisms that shape the lives, opportunities, and agency of others. When Maria notes that Shinji, the fisherman, perhaps doesn't "want" to be out on the boat every day because it is a routine, Alissa directs the class's attention to the fact that Shinji has a "master" and therefore that he lives as a subordinate to the will of another person.

The lesson also illustrates the teacher's clear role in providing explicit instruction and support—and how this is balanced with a focus on students' assessed needs and the contributions they are able to make as members of the learning community. Throughout the lesson, students' contributions are valued and built upon, and Alissa honors students' ideas by using them to develop the content of instruction and a platform from which to engage every student in intensive thinking work with the literature. Students who struggle with reading also received support during the lesson because they could listen to Alissa's reading of the text, see how she—and other students—thought about the text and the inquiry and could engage at any level with their own thoughts and ideas. Alissa's focus on the skill of reading for inquiry and on strategies for navigating text provided multiple ways for students to access the learning as readers, writers, and thinkers.

Phase 3: Helping Students Extend Their Ideas in Writing After Reading

As part of their work in using the inquiry process, students use a writer's notebook (Bomer, 1995) to explore their thinking. Once they have finished their reading of their novels and tracking their inquiry while reading, they synthesize a response to their inquiry question into the form of a thesis for an essay or extended response. Mini-lessons in this phase of the unit therefore focus on how to synthesize one's thinking about the question, formulate a response, and discuss findings from text to illustrate a thesis. To demonstrate what this process looks like, we will examine how one student, Paloma, developed her thesis and extended response over the course of the unit.

At the beginning of the unit, Alissa asked students to write about situations in their lives and the world around them that raised questions they might want to pursue. In the following entry, Paloma discusses how her experience with a personal relationship led her to raise questions about gender and power and how this caused her to revisit Ibsen's *A Doll's House* with a new lens:

> Last year I noticed a routine with my boyfriend and I. I was constantly trying to fix him, and make known the things he did wrong, and this resulted in him getting sad and making me feel bad for what I had said to him. In this way, he had control over me. Although current day it is common for women to have dominance over their men, I believe that my feeling of dominance in the relationship made me more vulnerable. This is because I had that label of the dominant figure [so] I was blinded to the actual situation. I also noticed that where I could control things such as places we went and things we did, he could control my emotions. From all this, I began to wonder why he would feel the need to control my emotions. In what way did he benefit by hurting me? Was there an underlying fear he had?
>
> I wondered what the literary characters might shed on these questions, and wondered whether I could track this hidden control— and where this need to control came from. Visiting "The Doll's House," I first noticed Nora's fear of being insecure. As she is married to Torvald, the reader may receive subtle hints of Nora's obsession with being well off. This insecurity leads to the feeling that she needs to have control.
>
> Later we see Nora's process of gaining control. It seems that Torvald talked to Nora as if she were inferior, and since he was given his dominant label, being bank manager, he allows himself to become more vulnerable to Nora. Perhaps this vulnerability comes from thinking that she couldn't possibly control him.

As Paloma and other students learned how to read for their inquiry, they began to track the connections they made to their inquiry. Students' thinking work at this stage took the form of adhesive notes with short responses, personal thoughts, and new questions related to their guiding question. This in-process writing is critically important, as it reflects students' thinking with text and ideas over time. In order to elaborate on and develop ideas in writing, students were then asked to construct extended responses using their adhesive notes as a jumping-off point.

Because personal inquiry work focuses on developing students' thinking processes and purposes, writing mini-lessons in Phase 3 focused on *how* to develop the inquiry in writing as a means to synthesize how we think about a question over time and across the reading process. Writing in the notebook during Phase 2 of the study emphasizes writing as thinking—not drafting. Alissa's students learned to develop an exploratory stance toward their personal and text connections, using the notebook to develop new questions and allow new lines of thinking to emerge. This represented a significant intellectual shift for many students, whose experiences with writing often tended to be more task-oriented and perfunctory than exploratory.

In their notebooks, students developed their inquiry questions, wrote about personal connections to those questions, and gathered examples from their books that related to them. After reflecting on her experiences and the questions that most mattered to her—and pertained to her text—Paloma worked to develop her overarching question. She also crafted smaller questions as part of the process of narrowing and clarifying her inquiry (see Figure 4.6).

While reading, students gathered and reflected on passages from their texts that helped them form a thesis in response to their inquiry. Students' notebook writing drew from their lives and experiences, while also helping them exercise skills for applying their ideas to the texts they read in ways that remained accountable to the texts themselves. In the excerpts from Paloma's notebook shown in Figures 4.6 and 4.7, we see her working through the process of developing and tying her ideas to *A Doll's House*. We also see her approximating the use of academic language, which Alissa explicitly taught as part of her work with students during instruction in Phase 3.

As students work with the material of their thoughts and lives, they grapple with the bigger questions that literature can help us to explore. Paloma's inquiry is significant not only because it helped her become a better reader of ideas but also because we see her striving to make sense of how power and

Figure 4.6. Paloma's Notebook Entry to Develop Her Inquiry Question

How much do we allow fear to control our lives? And what might change if it didn't influence our decisions?

Questioning the inquiry: ✗ = chosen questions!

✗ • what causes the fear?
✗ • How did the decision effect the character?
   • Is it natural fear, or psychological?
   • How do we allow bravery to overcome fear and 'why?
   • How much of an influence does fear have?
   • How does this fear vary based on culture age etc.
✗ • Why do we allow fear to control our lives?
   • why do we fear?

Figure 4.7. Excerpt of Paloma's Notebook Entry Connecting *A Doll's House* to Her Inquiry

```
p-34 :  " Well, yes, it really is very funny to think that
we — that Torvald has so much power over so many
people. "

Here we see Nora doubt Torvald's dominance.
She is discussing Torvald's overall position as
bank manager, while finding it amusing that
he can control all those people.  We have yet
to understand what feeds Nora's sense of control
over Torvald.  Nora's dialogue with Dr. Rank
remained normal until the break of hesitance
where she shifts "we" to "Torvald"..has so
much power.  Does Nora's fear of insecurity cause
her to control Torvald?  What might Ibsen be
saying about fear and how it relates to the
spousal dominance between Nora & Torvald.  Ibsen
begins this passage with Nora's humorous to
emphasize her views on her husband's power.
One might infer that Nora finds it humorously
how she can control Torvald, who is this powerful
figure in control of numerous people.
```

fear work in relationships and how gender roles play out in real life. Her inquiry holds the potential to inform her life by empowering her to have healthier relationships and to question how people position and control one another through socially constructed notions of gender.

In Paloma's final essay, we can see the echoes of her reading and inquiry process as it developed over the course of the unit. Challenging the notion that Nora's character is powerless, she writes:

> Henrik Ibsen's play, *The Doll House*, is a text of many possible interpretations as to whom Ibsen may have intended as the "Doll." Although one cannot fully comprehend the marital customs of Ibsen's time, one could perceive that, in the time of the late 1800's, the stereotypical figure of dominance was the husband. Wives often did as their husbands demanded, almost as if playing a childish game of house, a typical "doll wife," but I argue there is a hidden control possessed by

this less dominant figure. So who is the "doll" in Henrik Ibsen's play? By comparing the diction between his characters Nora and Torvald, the reader can see how Ibsen challenges us to reevaluate our perception of spousal control to differ from the common stereotype of the time.

Paloma's writing reflects her developing skills as an analytical reader, writer, and thinker. Through her exploration of the role of power in gender relationships, she also demonstrates engagement in inquiry from which social justice work can grow. The processes of reading and writing, taught explicitly through the work of the personal inquiry unit, provided her and her classmates with the supportive instruction needed to develop literacy tools for personally and socially meaningful work.

CONCLUSION

As illustrated through Alissa's classroom, students' own funds of knowledge can become a starting point for learning to read with greater depth and significance, giving students tools to use texts and ideas in potentially transformative ways. Chino, whose work formed the basis of the sample lesson in this chapter, described in an interview how his reading changed as a result of the approach that Alissa used in the personal inquiry unit:

> In my junior year, I did a lot of searching for ideas for the teacher, or searching for ideas that the class may have [come up with] as a whole, instead of things that I was interested in. And I found that now that I know I can use my interests to search for stuff, now as [a] senior, if something's interesting me then right away I'll take that idea and try to look more into it and follow up on it. . . . So I'd say that this [work in Alissa's class] was the foundation of actually starting to take better notes and looking into things that I'm interested in.

Like many high school students, Chino's lack of a personal purpose for reading had led him to engage in reading as a narrow task in search of "answers" instead of relevant meaning, or to rely on the interpretations and ideas of others (most often the teacher) rather than on developing his own ideas and interpretations of text. The personal inquiry approach helped him learn *how* to make his reading relevant and, in so doing, to become better at finding and nurturing his own ideas. Through deliberate instruction in personal inquiry, students exercise the right to their own ideas by gaining the tools to access those ideas in the first place. This is exactly what socially just teaching aspires to do.

CHAPTER FIVE

When Things Don't Work Right

Challenges and Opportunities for Socially Just Reading

LITTLE MOMENTS IN THE classroom are big: Students' reading, discussion, and inter-actions in the classroom can complicate even the most ardent efforts at socially just teaching. The texts students read in school, and the meanings they make from them, not only can raise issues and awareness of social justice concepts but also can serve to reproduce oppressive meanings and relationships. This chapter focuses on how reading work in the classroom can serve as an important site for helping students develop ways of reading and thinking that support social jus-tice objectives. As an important part of our teaching practice, we can continually study students' responses to reading as a means to inform our work and how we frame learning opportunities in equitable and empowering ways.

INQUIRING INTO STUDENTS' READING AS A MATTER OF SOCIAL JUSTICE

In this chapter, we will use several lenses for analyzing classroom reading events in order to make sense of the relationship between students' reading and the work of enacting a socially just pedagogy. To explore this area of practice in greater depth, Chapters 5 and 6 will focus on the story of the challenges faced by one classroom teacher, Melissa Baxter, who sought to engage students in learn-ing about issues of race as a matter of social justice. Because Melissa's classroom was the site for my dissertation research, I came to know her and her students well, and their case will enable us to apply lenses for analyzing classroom dis-course and interaction in order to consider how we might assess classroom con-texts in any time and place for the seeds of socially just teaching and learning.

Questions and Observations to Guide Analysis of Students' Reading

Classroom instruction and interaction are complex processes that seldom follow a prescribed and predictable path. Making sense of what is happening in a given classroom requires that we focus our observations so that we can see the possibilities and implications for social justice. The following questions and guidelines offer a way to see what is happening for students as readers and learners:

Inquiry 1: What meanings are students (individually and collectively) making?

- How do these meanings reinforce, resist, or complicate Discourses (Gee, 1999) that sustain dominant ideologies and relationships of power?
- What are some implications of those meanings for socially just teaching and learning?

The texts we use with students provide content and ideas that can promote thinking about social justice. Yet all readers bring their lived lives and experiences to the work of reading, and the meaning students make develop through their transactions with the text and interactions with other readers in the classroom context. Students may make meanings that contradict the message(s) of a text, and may resist or refigure the meanings in a text to fit their own understandings and purposes.

Inquiry 2: How are students making meaning (individually and collectively)?

- What processes and background knowledge do students use to make sense of texts and ideas?
- What logic do students employ in their thinking?
- What relationships of power in the classroom are shaping—and shaped by—students' meaning making?
- What implications for socially just teaching and learning can we draw from students' meaning-making process ?

When we try to make sense of how students are reading, we want to consider what aspects of a text students pay attention to, what cognitive strategies they do and don't use, and how the classroom context of their reading—especially their classroom interactions—works to shape the meanings they make. The more we understand about how students make meaning from their reading, the better we understand who they are as people, how they think, and what matters to them. Understanding students' reading processes also enables us to better assess them as learners and judge what skills and strategies they employ as they make sense of texts and ideas. Based on the above inquiries, Figure 5.1 offers some ways to guide our observation of students' classroom reading work.

Figure 5.1. Look-Fors in Classroom Reading Work

When we observe classroom discourse and interactions around reading, we can listen and look for . . .

- Voices and ideas that dominate or are taken up by the group
- Voices and ideas that are marginalized
- Consensus or outliers around ideas and meanings
- How students position themselves and one another in the classroom
- If and how students form alliances in the classroom
- Whether and how students' meaning making enacts Discourses and interactions that sustain oppressive ideas and relationships

As we visit Melissa Baxter's classroom, we will practice using the preceding inquiries to analyze and reflect on the implications for socially just pedagogy in light of students' readings, interactions, and meaning making in a particular time and place. While the inquiries and tools for analysis may be universal, the contexts in which students learn are not. By examining particular problems of practice in socially just teaching, I hope to empower educators to make sense of their own students in context, and in so doing, to find a way forward.

PUTTING SOCIALLY JUST READING IN CONTEXT

Melissa Baxter's Language Arts Class at Eastman High

If you were to walk into the lunchroom at Eastman High School[1] on any given day, you would see a striking pattern of color: Along the walls of the rectangular cafeteria, a solid line of Black bodies; in the middle of the room, a sea of White. Loosened from the restrictions of classroom seating arrangements, Eastman High students often reverted to color-coded social and spatial arrangements by race. Although students often claimed that they "got along" and evidence of social integration could be seen at times in hallways and classrooms, segregated patterns of behavior and social selection nevertheless carried over into the classroom.

Eastman, located in the urban fringe of Detroit, is a comprehensive public high school serving approximately 700 students, of whom 35% were on free and reduced-price lunch. The school demographics during the 2005–2006 school year (when the study was conducted) were largely representative of two racial and ethnic groups: 56% of students identified themselves as Black/African American, 41% self-identified as White, 2% as Hispanic, and 1% as Pacific Islander. During an in-school interview at lunchtime, Sparky and her friend Bea (both White and female), discussed the racialized patterns that shaped their lives as students at Eastman:[2]

> Bea (W): We're pretty segregated here, too, like most of the people—
>   Black people sit on this side and White people—
> Laura (W): At lunch?
> Bea: Well, in classrooms, at lunch—
> Sparky (W): —everywhere.
> Bea: We segregate ourselves.
> Laura: Well, I'd kind of noticed that, 'cause every time I go down in
>   the lunchroom, all the White students are in the middle, and all the
>   African American students are along the side. People just do that by
>   habit, or choice, or—?
> Bea: They just sit with people they feel comfortable with. I wouldn't
>   want to go to a table full of African Americans and—just—sit down
>   and eat and start talking. I'd feel uncomfortable.
> (Small-group interview, June 16, 2005)

The girls' observations reflect the racial history of the community. Grandville, located in the greater Detroit area, had historically been characterized by tension and conflict between Black and White residents. I visited Eastman regularly as a researcher in Melissa Baxter's 9th-grade English language arts class, which Sparky attended. Although the term in which I observed Melissa's class was marked by only one large-scale fight, in which six students were arrested in connection with a gun incident, students and staff noted that the history of the school was significantly marked by racial fights in which groups of Black and White students pitted themselves against each other. And although Sparky noted that some students had "friends in different races," the more enduring boundaries of segregation and racial identity remained visibly intact. As one Mexican American student who was new to the school told Melissa, "In this school, I have to be Black or White. So I choose Black."

In this school context, how do we imagine teaching for social justice? Seeing that race shaped students' lives in school every day, Melissa sought ways to help her students make sense of race and discrimination as a matter of justice. She took a stance of building students' learning around issues that mattered in their community and, therefore, considered how students' reading might provide opportunities for exploring how race "works" to afford inequitable access to opportunities and resources. To do this, Melissa did what many of us do: She chose texts for students to read that were intended to foster discussion and learning around issues of social justice, pertaining especially to issues of race and class.

In the following scenarios from Melissa's class, we will focus on ways to study students' responses to reading in order to see challenges and opportunities for socially just teaching. While I will address the ways in which the context for this class posed particular challenges, the problems of practice illustrated here can emerge whenever we engage students in reading together. As we visit Melissa's classroom, consider how these lenses might help you make sense of opportunities for socially just teaching in your school or classroom context. How and when have you seen these problems of practice with students? In Chapter 6, we will examine some strategies to address the challenges explored here.

Lenses for Analysis of Students' Reading Work

Lens 1: Positioning Readers and Texts. Given the context in which her students lived and learned, Melissa, a White teacher, considered how the texts students read for language arts might draw on issues of race in order to help them make sense of racial segregation and conflict in their own school and community. Like teachers in many districts I've worked with, she also had to navigate the demands of required curriculum: Shakespeare's *Romeo and Juliet* and Hansberry's *A Raisin in the Sun* were not only texts the district expected her to teach; they were also what was available in the book room. She considered how these texts, as well as others she chose throughout the semester, could engage students in dialogue and understanding about race, class, and conflict to help them transform their relationships with each other in school. Once the texts were put to use, however, what became increasingly important was not only the texts themselves, but how students responded to them and what opportunities were created for developing students' critical and transformative literacy.

The concept of positioning offers an important lens for thinking about how we can help students read for social justice. In a given classroom interaction, students may position themselves and others as powerful or impotent, smart or stupid, cool or uncool. They may also draw on stereotypes and oppressive relationships to position students or groups as subordinate. When we consider the classroom context for reading, we can notice how students' interactions with each other serve to position their identities in ways that may disrupt or reproduce social hierarchies and relations of power. As teachers, our language can also position students as readers, learners, and human beings. Consider, for example, this interaction between Melissa and several students during a class discussion:

Lynette (AA): Like you can't change people's attitudes of being racist. Like if you go into Joy OK [a local store], the owner will follow you around . . .

Randall (AA): Yeah. I don't like her.

Melissa (W): Is there a way to make rules, or to make people treat each other in a way that protects people's rights? Is there a way for me to make Scott, for example, treat each of you in a way that protects each individual's rights?

Randall (AA): No.

Christopher (AA): No.

Randall (AA): No. It's never gonna be fair.

(Field notes, April 19, 2005)

In this brief example, notice how Melissa takes up students' ideas about race and social change as a focus for inquiry. As part of a class discussion about the American Dream in the context of students' reading of the play *A Raisin in the Sun*, Melissa enabled students to bring and build on their experiences as raced, classed, and cultured human beings. She could have challenged or glossed over students' assertions. Instead, she positioned them to become inquirers, to probe rather than simply accept their experiences and ideas as an endpoint for their learning.

Just as we can say that students' identities can be positioned by others, we can think of texts as positioning identities and readers also. In the play *A Raisin in the Sun*, for example, the writer Lorraine Hansberry has created characters whose identities as African Americans, as middle-class people, and as residents of Chicago in the 1950s figure prominently in the story and reflect the author's portrayal of how and why those aspects of their identity matter for pursuing the American Dream. The identities of the characters are positioned relative to one another within the narrative to illustrate how race and power shape people's lives and opportunities. We see the White realtor, Mr. Lindner, as he meets with the family to discuss why they cannot buy the home of their dreams in an all-White neighborhood. We listen as Walter and Ruth try to make sense of their life together based on their understandings of who they are as a Black man and a Black woman in America. As we watch or read the play, the text creates a position for us as readers as well: We are observers who can see how the family's dreams can die like "a raisin in the sun" when their economic opportunities are determined by a system that favors Whiteness and oppresses African Americans. To make sense of how the social context shapes the family's experience, we must assume a level of objectivity in our stance as readers.

Because writers write with certain audiences and purposes in mind, texts can create what we call *subject positions*—certain stances or identities we need to assume as readers of a given text in order to make meaning from it (Kress, 1989; Ong, 2002) To think of it another way, we can consider, while reading, the following question: Who does the writer of this text think that I am? Who is the text designed to address, and what does it assume about the audience?

Students can at times perceive and respond to these subject positions while reading in the classroom.

Yet readers also choose the positions they take when reading a text. Because we interact with texts as human beings who make meaning about identities and social experience, teachers need to consider how the identities portrayed in texts and the subject positions they offer may influence students' engagement with the text in the classroom. To complicate things further, *how* teachers choose and use texts with students can serve to position the text—and student readers—as well. Such positionings can help us make sense of students' responses, such as that of a Native American high school student, Dawn, who complained that her school's emphasis on a culturally relevant curriculum emphasizing Native history was "depressing" to her. "All we read about is how we [got screwed over] by White people. It's depressing. Why can't we read about something else?" Although her teachers sought fervently to help students understand their own history in light of social justice, Dawn's response can help us think about how texts might be chosen and used in ways that students experience as empowering rather than depressing.

Working with texts in the classroom therefore requires that we consider students' identities, the identities and positions offered through a given text, and how students' reading and discussion might help them construct socially just meanings and relationships. But the alchemy that occurs with readers and texts in context is never a known variable; this requires, then, that teachers continually attend and respond to the interaction among readers, texts, and contexts (Moje, Dillon, & O'Brien, 2000). With literature in particular, the challenge is to consider how the text, as a work of art, might affect us and provoke us to new thoughts and ideas. Reading has the power to move us beyond experiencing texts in which we consider only the identities and positions that match our experiences or current ways of thinking and being. To read in ways that support a socially just agenda is to not only read deeply to understand our own communities and experiences, but to read diversely, and for diversity, as well. Texts may at times challenge readers with subject positions that are uncomfortable and challenging but necessary for critical analysis and understanding of how injustices are constructed through the macro- and microstructures of our social world.

Put another way, I am arguing that students' responses to texts and the positions from which they read are just as important—if not more so—than the texts we choose for the explicit teaching of content relevant to social justice. Even when notions of race, class, or gender are not explicitly mentioned in the text, they may nevertheless emerge as students make meaning. In Melissa's class, students' racialized responses surfaced not only from the texts that Melissa independently selected for the class to read but also from texts that were part of the 9th-grade curriculum and considered "classics." Students often made racial comments and connections to texts and, at times, drew inferences that explicitly named issues of race and justice. Lee, an African American student, marked the characters in *Romeo and Juliet* as raced, noting to me during class one day that "Juliet had to be a White girl because no Black woman would kill herself over a man!" In this example, Lee views the play's themes of romantic love, gender roles, and power in light of his racial identity and experience, calling into question the cultural basis for the narrative and its perceived universality. Students' marking of the text therefore went beyond merely labeling or identifying the author or characters as raced to making meaning about race and racial identity.

In another example, students marked Hansberry's *A Raisin in the Sun* as a text for and about African Americans, leading Scott, a White student, to complain that the play was "racist" because there "weren't enough White characters besides the racist White guy." In the play, the primary White character is the realtor Lindner, who attempts to prevent the African American characters from moving into an all-White neighborhood. We can understand Scott's treatment of the text as "racist" as his taking a reader position based on White racial representation. This kind of reading position creates the potential, however, for Scott (W) to ignore or dismiss important aspects of the text because of his resistance to the representation of White characters—even when the portrayal of the White character is historically accurate and thematically necessary for exploring central issues in the text.

And herein lies the rub: When students mark and respond to texts as raced, classed, and gendered, this can position students themselves and the meanings they make in ways that complicate the goals of socially just pedagogy. When students make claims in the classroom about what counts as "White" or "Black," "gay" or "straight," they not only may complicate the content and purpose for reading to make sense of social justice, but also may shut down possibilities for other ways of thinking or being. Their responses can then further position other students in the classroom in ways that become socially and personally limiting, rather than liberating. These moments of classroom interaction therefore provide important sites for reflection and action. Figure 5.2 offers a starting point for reflection, using the lens of positioning.

Lens 2: Alliances. Before I began researching in Melissa's classroom, she told me the story of a class discussion she'd held the previous term, with a different class, in which the students debated their positions on capital punishment. During the activity, she had asked students to physically move themselves to different sides of the classroom to represent their position on the issue: Those who were "for" stood on one side, those "against" stood on the other. As she watched in surprise, students divided the room straight down the middle, with the White students clustering in favor of capital punishment

Figure 5.2. Reflecting on Instructional Practice

Consider the texts you have used to teach for social justice in the classroom:

- What groups and identities are represented in these texts and how are they represented, especially in relation to other groups?
- How do these texts address students as readers? What kind of person does the text assume the reader to be?
- How are *you*, as the teacher, making meaning from the text? What identities are you drawing from as you make meaning, and how might this relate to or differ from the ways that students make meaning?
- What conversations do you hope to foster by using a given text? What assumptions might you be making about how students will respond to or interact with the text?

Consider how students engage with and respond to texts used in the classroom:

- How have you (the teacher) created opportunities for students to respond to text and make meaning?
- What ideas stand out in students' responses and what are the implications for social justice?
- How do students position one another as people in the classroom, particularly during reading (e.g., smart, not smart; capable, inept; powerful, disempowered; Black, White; male, female; gay, straight).?
- Try recording some of your class discussions of reading, listening for how students position the text and one another. Or write about a particular class discussion that was confusing or troubling—where students responded differently from what was expected. As you revisit what happened during a given classroom episode, what aspects of the text do students connect with—or reject? Develop an inquiry to investigate their responses.

and the Black students aligned against. Melissa was struck by the racial split in the room and publicly noted it to the class. When she tried to engage students in a discussion about it, however, she was met with silence from the White students and dismissive laughter from the Black students: "We all have family members in jail!" they replied. And the discussion ended.

Melissa had not intended her class activity as an investigation into issues of race, and yet the alliances and rifts within the classroom, for a moment, became painfully visible. Even when she sought to help students examine and discuss this issue, however, Melissa was often faced with both the need for and the challenge of response. Considering this example, was it better to raise the issue of race with students directly, and risk negatively positioning African American students or raising painful family issues? Could that interaction have served to further reinforce stereotypes of African

Americans? And how could she engage students in a critical examination of the way in which White privilege and racial prejudice may shape their views and lives?

In response to the power relationships and hierarchies in the classroom context, students may act strategically to form alliances and thereby to position themselves most advantageously within social relationships. When we notice the power dynamics within a given classroom, we may see students' alliances form along axes of race, gender, and socioeconomic status, as the preceding story demonstrates. These alliances can then shape students' reading and meaning making in the classroom in ways that have important implications for socially just teaching.

I define an *alliance* as a collaboration among two or more individuals—through their talk or actions—that serves to help them define power and positions in a social context such as the classroom. Alliances can therefore serve strategic purposes for defining, preserving, and defending identities and social positions. My intention here is not to define all social interactions in the classroom as strategically motivated in this way, but to consider how the concept of alliances can be useful for understanding how students navigate the social worlds of the classroom and how alliances can shape critical moments in socially just teaching and learning.

Alliances are important to students' reading and learning in two ways: First, meanings constructed in the whole-class setting inform what knowledge and ideas "count"—both socially and academically (Santa Barbara Discourse Group, 1994). Because alliances help students to create a shared position relative to particular meanings and ideas, they may then control which meanings and ideas are heard, which are silenced, and how learning in the classroom is consequently shaped. Second, meanings formed through whole-class discussions, and the alliances formed around those meanings actively construct the histories of participation (Rogers, 2002) of the classroom—the story of who we are as a class, how we learn together, and what ideas and meanings are most valued. Alliances therefore have the potential to shape future interactions and meaning making in ways that can silence, restrain, or empower.

Within the classroom, students may forge social, cultural, and academic alliances along axes of difference such as race, class, gender, or ethnicity. We can observe these alliances by noticing how students organize themselves physically and socially, and in the kinds of meanings with which they align through their talk and participation. At times, for example, Melissa and I noticed her students lining up their participation and responses according to race and gender, often around reading and discussion activities.

In the following scene from the classroom, Melissa had introduced the concept of the American Dream, which figures thematically in *A Raisin in the Sun*. As part of their ongoing exploration of this idea, students discussed obstacles to their dreams in connection to the poem "Dreams," by Langston Hughes (1994), which reads as follows:

> Hold fast to dreams
>   for if dreams die
> Life is a broken-winged bird
>   that cannot fly.
> Hold fast to dreams
>   for when dreams go
> Life is a barren field
>   frozen with snow.

Students had read the poem and discussed it in small groups prior to engaging in large-group discussion, when the following conversation took place:

Randall (AA): People don't want to put work into their dreams.

Darius (AA): Sometimes it's not that, though. Sometimes people can try to hold you down.

Laura (W): Can you say more about what you mean?

Darius (AA): I know from personal experience, like with my dad. . . . He works in the hospital and he's trying to move up . . . to get a better job and it's like he has recommendations, but there's people tryin' to hold him down.

Laura (W): Why does he think people are trying to hold him down?

Darius (AA): My dad thinks it's because of race but I don't know.

Laura (W): Why does he think that it's because of race?

Several African American students: That's how they do us.

Several other African American students: *Mmmhmmm.*

Melissa (W): That's a fair statement.

(Field notes, February, 24, 2005)

This moment created interesting opportunities and challenges for socially just teaching. On the one hand, students raised awareness of the way in which race can serve as an institutionalized barrier to one's dreams. Although Darius expressed ambivalence about his father's assertion that other people can "hold you down" because of race, other African American students affirmed this idea. In so doing, they "engaged Whiteness" (Leonardo, 2004): They noted how Whiteness functions as a kind of "property" through which social benefits are conferred in structural and institutional ways (Harris, 1995; Ladson-Billings, 2004). In this interaction, the alliance ("us") created among several African American students also implicitly defined Whites as "them."

Although the class discussion of the text had not previously focused on race, Darius's connection to his father's experience created the possibility for racial meaning to be considered. And although Hughes is a Harlem Renaissance poet, his poem does not explicitly mention race as a subject or, more explicitly, as a limitation to dreams. Responding to the text, Darius used his father's experience of race to make sense of what makes dreams "die," and in doing so, illuminated how race could shape dreams, futures, and the academic present in which Darius was constructing his future self. Although Darius's response provided a powerful means for understanding the poem and arguably created the potential for critical reading and examination of racial power structures, the positioning of Whites as "them" may have contributed to the stalemate that followed. This may explain the White students' response, for although Melissa acknowledged African American students' assertion of the reality of racial oppression, White students remained silent in response to this idea and the conversation moved on to other subjects.

The point is not that Darius and other African American students should not name White privilege or Whiteness as issues for discussion, but that critical moments like these can have powerful consequences and that teachers need to respond constructively to facilitate students' learning by using their responses, rather than ignoring or glossing over them. Students' silence surrounding the issue of race in shaping social futures can lead to troubling consequences if White students resist an examination of the role(s) of Whiteness and White people in perpetuating racism or if African American students see race as a limiting factor that contributes to a sense of futility in their academic aspirations and efforts.

Such moments can potentially contribute to troubling social and academic consequences for students. After all, how much can socially just pedagogy really do to address racial power relations when White students do not engage in analyzing those relations with their African American peers? Without true cross-racial conversation that both acknowledges race and provides a means for students to productively learn from and about each other, transformative pedagogy is not possible. In socially just teaching practice, we can work with *and* against students' alliances to foster the conditions needed for critical reading and transformation. Chapter 6 will outline several strategies toward that end. Figure 5.3 offers questions for reflection, using the lens of alliances and their implications for socially just teaching.

Lens 3: Patterns of Meaning—Hegemony, Resistance, and Silence.
Another problem of practice lies in the extent to which students make meanings that sustain naturalized social orders and hierarchies that are unjust. The habit of studying students' discourse and their written work, a critical aspect of socially just practice, allows us to make sense of the patterns of meaning that students bring to and construct in the classroom. Because we must continually respond to students and to their developing understanding, we examine

Figure 5.3. Seeing Alliances in the Classroom

As part of a teaching practice focused on social justice, we can look and listen for the following:

- How students physically and socially arrange themselves in the room
  - » Are there insiders and outsiders?
  - » What alliances are formed and why?
  - » Who is included or excluded?
- What groups or identities students align themselves with
  - » How do students identify themselves in relation to one another?
  - » How do different groups in the classroom interact?
  - » What does it mean to students to belong to a given group or to form a given alliance?
- How students position themselves and their ideas relative to one another
  - » Do some topics or ideas create fault lines in the classroom?
  - » What ideas and meanings do students regard as most influential or important?
  - » What ideas or meanings are left out or marginalized?
  - » How do students' ideas form the basis for alliances in the classroom?
  - » What are the implications of students' ideas and alliances for socially just teaching?

student work to consider *how* students, as individuals and as members of social groups, make meaning and *what* meanings they are constructing. Therein lie important seeds for social justice work.

When examining students' written work and reflecting on their discussions in Melissa's class, I noticed several important patterns. First, as mentioned earlier, Melissa and I both saw a tendency for White students to become silent when issues of race were engaged during class discussion. Students' written responses to *Raisin* further revealed differences between the meanings that White and African American students were making with the play. When discussing the racial identities of Black characters, African American students' responses commonly expressed themes of struggle, strength, and pride in their interpretations. Carla's (AA) analysis of the character of Ruth (AA) in *A Raisin in the Sun* exemplifies the theme of struggle:

> Ruth is a very strong Black woman who has been through so much in her life. . . . She is always cooking and cleaning up after someone and then she has to deal with her husband Walter Lee. He is always talking about investing in a liquor store with his Mama from her check . . . . Ruth's life has a lot to do with the American Dream because she is always doing what's right. And in another way her life doesn't have to do with the American Dream because she is always cleaning up after someone. (*Raisin in the Sun* essay)

In this response, Carla did not simply assert that Ruth was a strong woman; rather, her assertion that "Ruth is a very strong Black woman" directly linked her strength and her Blackness together. Carla further related Ruth's strength to a sense of struggle, portraying the character as someone who had "been through so much in her life" yet who perseveres. Across the responses of African American male and female case study readers, students usually linked this theme of "strength" to Black characters.

The African American boys in the class also emphasized this theme with reference to Black men, as in Harvey's (AA) written analysis of the character Walter (AA) in *Raisin*:

> I learned [that] when it's time to step up and made things right, Walter the person. (Written response, April 29, 2005)

> See, Walter realized at the end that what was important to him is his family. His American Dream wasn't the liquor store. So he made a choice to buy the house and move in. It made him feel good for his family to be proud of him. (*Raisin in the Sun* essay)

Why might these themes matter for African American students? In considering the answer to this question, let's contrast African American students' readings and interpretations of the character of Walter (AA) with White students' readings. Although African American students' responses strongly emphasized the themes of pride and strength, thereby figuring Walter in positive terms as an African American man, their White counterparts in the classroom made no mention of pride in their reading and emphasized very different qualities for this African American male character. Figure 5.4 shows samples of the White students' responses to Walter that reflect their dominant interpretations of him in their written work.

The White students' reading responses reflected an interpretation of Walter that overwhelmingly represented him in negative terms. Even Scott's reading of Walter, which could be seen as neutral, emphasized what Walter *wanted* and *lacked*: "the American Dream, money, and . . . family support." None of these interpretations portrayed Walter as strong or proud, contrasting sharply with the African American students' readings. My point here is not that the White students' interpretations were necessarily "wrong," for the character of Walter is complex and flawed, as are all the main characters. Rather, their reading of that African American male character emphasized negative qualities that together constructed a more stereotypical portrait of him as an African American male while completely ignoring the character's resilient and positive qualities in the text. The White students' reading thus stood in sharp contrast with the African American students' readings, which afforded a more hopeful, transformative

Figure 5.4. White Students' Written Responses to the Character of Walter in *A Raisin in the Sun*

White Case Study Reader	Representative Responses to the Character of Walter
Dan	"I learned that Walter is a very emotional person." Dan chose the following terms to describe Walter and provided evidence for each descriptor: "angry: In every scene he is hollering at somebody." "irresponsible: Gets drunk." "gullible: Gave money to someone to buy something."
Sparky	"Mama's son Walter was greedy and didn't care about anyone but himself."
Scott	"What's poor, colored, and trys [sic] real hard to get ahead in life? A thirty-five-year-old African American man by the name of Walter Lee Younger." "He [Walter] wants the American Dream, money, and he wants some family support."

view of Walter as an African American man who maintained his dignity and fought for his family despite the odds.

Assuming reader positions along the lines of race (and at times gender) may have allowed students to focus on certain aspects of a text at the expense or exclusion of others. This could then result in a kind of partial reading—one in which students sought to harmonize elements of a text to their existing racial schema, rather than to challenge or complicate that schema. This kind of reading practice poses several challenges to socially just pedagogies. First, it enables students to ignore aspects of a text that they may not wish to "deal with," resulting in selective rather than comprehensive and thorough reading. Second, proficient readers are able to approach a text with an open-minded, objective disposition and are willing to abandon ideas and existing schemas as they acquire new information and develop their thinking (Blau, 2003). Without the appropriate challenges and supports to develop critical habits of thinking, students are at risk of becoming partial readers, seeing only what they want to see in a text. And without engaged, critical reading, the project of teaching for social justice falls short.

PUTTING IT ALL TOGETHER: EXAMINING A CRITICAL MOMENT IN THE CLASSROOM

Noticing and working against oppressive Discourses and habits of thinking becomes more challenging when students enact meanings during class discussions that beg an immediate response. Issues of positioning and alliance-building come into play as students forward habits of thinking and meaning making that may sustain apathy for the status quo rather than informed social consciousness and the seeds of social action. In the next example, we'll examine a longer segment of class discussion to see how students' reading and interactions pose challenges for transformative pedagogy.

As part of their work in a unit of study on essay writing, Melissa chose to have the class read a student essay from the book *Reading, Writing, and Rising Up: Teaching About Social Justice and the Power of the Written Word* (Christensen, 2000). The essay, "Tar Baby," explores race and color privilege from the perspective of a young African American woman who experienced discrimination because of her darker skin color. Melissa selected the text as a means to address some of the racial tensions and dynamics she observed every day. An excerpt of the essay reads as follows:

> During the Atlantic slave trade, Africans on plantations across the South were treated like animals. They were thought to be less than human, but even within this undignified category, they were further classified by color. It started that far back: When all Blacks were nothing, still color was an issue. The lighter you were, the closer to the house you toiled, and the less work you did. In those days, there was no beauty in color, and if you had some, you were destined to be working way out in the field. Even today, I see the remnants of the Field nigga, House nigga syndrome. . . .
>
> In most magazines you pick up, you can find at least one African-American woman, but usually she is a little light-eyed biracial girl who does little to represent women of color. Be gone with those tiny waisted, no-hip-having heifers. Bring on the models who range in color from caramel to dark chocolate . . . (from "Tar Baby," by Kahlliah Joseph, in Christensen, 2000, p. 70)

Asked to discuss their responses to "Tar Baby," Harvey (AA) and several of his peers (also African American) wrestled with the complex relationship between race and color:

> Harvey (AA): I was wondering why, um, she [the author] doesn't understand that people of her own race put her down, but other people [in other races] see her beauty.
> Melissa (W): That's a question.
> *[Harvey (AA) said he didn't understand part of the text, and indicated that he was looking at the last line of the text in the second-to-last paragraph. He read the passage aloud haltingly. As he did so, Carla laughed, presumably at his struggle to read.]*

Harvey (AA): How can someone of her own race tease her about how
   she looks?
Darius (AA): But they're not the same color.
Marie (AA): They're the same race.
Harvey (AA): Yeah.
Randall (AA): That's a nice question.
(Field notes and audio transcription, March 14, 2005)

Harvey's question addressed a central issue in the text, namely, that of
discrimination against dark-skinned African Americans by those with whiter
skin, including lighter-skinned African Americans. The writer speaks to a racial power dynamic wherein the possession of Whiteness, even by degrees,
privileges some people and groups over others. In part, Melissa chose the text
because of students' ongoing and explicit reference to skin color as a means for
social marking and positioning. Throughout the essay, the writer discusses her
own experiences of oppression as a darker-skinned African American. Melissa
intended the reading of the text as a means for exploring White privilege and
how it related to students' everyday lives and experiences.

Hoping to engage students in making connections to their own lives, Melissa initiated further conversation with students by asking if anyone had had
an experience of racial labeling similar to that described by the author of "Tar
Baby." Carla (AA), who also had darker skin, described her own experience of
being called "Blackie." As she told the story, however, she laughed to mini-
mize the importance of it. This then became a kind of joke among Carla (AA),
Marie (AA), and Lynette (AA). In an attempt to refocus students' attention
on the issues of social justice raised in the text, Melissa responded as follows:

Melissa: Do you think darker-skinned women get left out of things?

Marie (AA) pointed out there was a "bald-headed model" in the magazines
who was making a "lot of money." She offered this as disconfirming evidence
that darker-skinned Black women face discrimination. "There's like two of
them," she announced. Seated together at one side of the circle, Carla (AA),
Lynette (AA), and Ellen (AA) continued to make fun of the conversation.
Jade's (AA) face remained serious. She raised her hand:

Jade (AA): I don't think this is funny, to be honest with you, because a
   lot of people have been discriminated against because of color.

Jade added that although some magazines feature dark-skinned models, in
many cases it was nevertheless true that dark-skinned women face discrimination. Carla responded as follows:

Carla (AA): It's not funny, but at the same time, you can't let it bother you.

As this discussion continued, the White students were not participating, and they did not appear to be overtly engaged in what was happening. In fact, they were not looking at the other students in the room.

Edward (AA) then entered the conversation, asserting that when students comment on each other's color, "that's just playing around." Jade tried to redirect the conversation to take the issue more seriously.

Jade (AA): People make fun of you for different things. . . . It can become serious. They can probably feel lesser than other people or it can hurt them.

Lynette (AA): I don't really think of it as racism. . . . because people at this school make fun of people's color then turn around and be friends with a dark-skinned person.

Bob (AA): I think it's just blazin'.

(Field notes and audio transcription, March 14, 2005)

Positioning, Alliances, and Consensus Meanings in Action

During this discussion, the African American (and primarily female) students noticeably engaged, and the White students noticeably disengaged. Asked as Black females to examine their own raced and gendered status, which was negatively positioned in the text (regardless of intent), the girls responded as a group and quickly chose sides.

The girls divided themselves according to position, representing the notion that it (race) "doesn't matter" on one side (with Carla, Lynette, and Marie) and that it does matter on the other side. Jade represented the outlier by insisting that the subject of racism against Black women be taken seriously in their discussion. Throughout this exchange, which lasted over 15 minutes, Carla, Lynette, and Marie consistently resisted Jade's appeals to the point of silencing her altogether. Carla, who on another occasion was identified by the other African American girls as "darker" than they were, argued adamantly against Jade's attempts to entertain the issue of skin color privilege as one that required reflection and social action.

The strength of students' alliance against Jade created an uneasy consensus in the classroom that racism did not merit social attention as a critical social issue and that students' race talk at the school site was "just blazin'" and "doesn't really matter." While students' subjective responses were not uniform, a sense of ambivalence toward the status quo nevertheless prevailed and was sustained through students' alliances in the classroom.

The few responses made by White students signaled their alignment with Carla and the others as well. John (W), for example, compared Carla's experience of being marked for her dark skin to White students' experiences, claiming that the issue of racial discrimination was "just like"the ways that Whites may comment on the color of one another's skin. "With us it's like Caspar versus tan," he said. In equalizing his experience with Carla's, John casts the issue of racial discrimination as an issue of mere teasing. By casting the issue in this light, John and the other White students helped to neutralize the meaning of racial oppression and effectively exempted themselves from the need to recognize the history of White racial oppression or to reflect on the ways in which Whiteness works to social advantage.

If we focus on the meanings students were collectively making, we can see Carla's assertion that "you can't let it bother you"constructs her as a subject, but one with limited power to affect the social world. Racial oppression is assumed as inevitable, and the"you" can only act in self-protection. The meaning that students make therefore constructs a kind of individualism (rather than collectivism) that undermines the possibility for social action or reform. The victim of racial oppression can only protect him- or herself from an intangible force—without responding to or altering the actual source or condition of oppression itself.

Seeing what happened "in color"reveals important aspects of the classroom dynamic represented above. The meanings Carla and her classmates made with the text are complicated by the fact that the other African American girls in the room, who identified and positioned themselves as lighter-skinned, also identified Carla as "dark." The meanings they made through discussion, then, can be seen to serve several purposes: (1) for Carla, to protect her social position by refuting the text's assertion that darker-skinned Black women have an inferior social position and therefore experience discrimination; (2) for the other African American females, to avoid claiming or recognizing the privileged color position of lighter skin (even as they claimed it); and (3) for White students, to silence the issues of White power and Black racial subordination such that they could avoid taking any social or individual responsibility for it.

Reading Effects of Class Discussion: Silencing Readers and Meanings

In a later conversation during an out-of-school interview, Jade examined the transcript of the preceding classroom exchange and expressed concern and confusion over her African American female peers' responses:

> I don't think a person should just make fun of like some people, because . . . somebody makin' fun of you because of something you can't change. . . .You can't control it, you can't change it, you know? That's your life. (August 22, 2005)

She noted that "making fun" of someone can have serious consequences: "And that's why some teens go through like a depression and stuff, and think about suicide and stuff." Jade's response, which separated her from her African American peers, contested the notion that race talk amounts to "making fun" and attempted to address the realities and social consequences of sustaining Discourses based on White privilege. But students' ambivalent response to racism and sexism reflects a larger uncertainty about the source of racial oppression and power and the limits of individual agency in asserting an autonomous identity.

Critical moments like this one deserve serious consideration, for they construct dangerous traps for students and teachers. Although students worked collectively to dismiss the importance of racial stratification, the ambivalent meaning they constructed neither made anyone or anything responsible for addressing racism nor gave African American female students any tools for addressing oppressive conditions or ideas. Instead, the notion that "it don't matter" remained the consensus in the room, in spite of Jade's efforts to raise awareness and engage her fellow students in more meaningful discussion.

This position of ambivalence, although it may have served to help students negotiate a sense of social constraint, nevertheless made the issue of racial subjection the responsibility only of the victim, leaving no clear avenue for social reform. Students' patterns of meaning making therefore functioned as means of resignation and social inaction, which inevitably left little hope for social transformation.

Although students' responses made sense in connection with their experiences of race in the school and community, the dynamics of classroom interaction also worked to silence particular aspects of texts and to silence readers who might have brought other meanings to whole-class reading. Typically, the girls in the room often chose not to share meanings or interpretations that could have potentially conflicted with dominant interpretations that were co-constructed by the class. In fact, the collective resistance to directly addressing race or gender oppression in the classroom acted to constrain the meanings available and created a space in which students who had experienced racial discrimination might become further marginalized.

Following the "Tar Baby" discussion illustrated above, I interviewed Jade outside of school to ascertain her thoughts about what had happened in that discussion and the role she had played. Her response shows how race— whether explicitly engaged or not—can shape students' school engagement, and not because of a perceived link between achievement and "acting White" or because of cultural factors, as some theories have suggested (Ogbu, 2003). Rather, Jade's response suggests that nonrecognition of students' racial realities and struggles may be an important reason for disengagement. In reflecting on what had happened in that discussion, Jade told me she had thought it was important to say something, but that it was difficult for her to do so:

I don't know because . . . you can't change people's minds when people
are disagreeing with you, so . . . I don't like to have to go through all
that and explain myself. . . . People take it like a joke, like, but like
Edward and all them start laughing, but it's still, I don't know . . . I didn't
understand. . . . Things are based upon color, and things, like if you're
dark skinned or brown, or . . . the color of cashmere . . . light-skinned
people make fun of dark-skinned people. . . . You don't laugh it off, you
know. (Interview, March 16, 2005)

Jade's conflicting assertions that "people should find out about it" and
alternately that "you can't change people's minds and people are disagreeing
with you, so . . . I don't like to have to go through all that" frames the dilemma
confronting teachers when critical moments in reading occur. When race is
present in the text, contexts, or readers' responses, teachers must choose to
either address the subject at hand or to allow it to go unaddressed. This is true
when other issues of identity (e.g., gender, ability, sexuality, ethnicity) surface
in students' reading as well. Both responses—addressing the issue or silencing
it—can create difficulties for students in the classroom, whose identities may
be at risk either way. I would argue, however, that teachers must own and
address the meanings students make about identity in their classrooms and
must effectively facilitate student talk that can elevate the level of students'
thinking, create opportunities for understanding, and make the classroom a
safe place for students of all identities. If this does not occur, if potentially
harmful meanings go unaddressed or unexplored, students like Jade are at
risk of being silenced and of disengaging for having to "go through all that."

Although students' discussion of "Tar Baby" foreclosed to the meaning
that race "doesn't matter" and that you "can't let it bother you," other readings
and positions like Jade's were not present in the discussion that might have
moved the class toward a more critical perspective and more transformative
outcomes. Here, for example, is Lynette's written response to "Tar Baby," written *before* she engaged in small- and large-group discussion:

I think this essay was very deep. She told the truth of what and how
people treat darker people than them. I see it every day happen to kids
and they don't do anything about it. (March 14, 2005)

Lynette's written response voices an idea and a stance toward the text that
was never heard or addressed in the context of whole-group discussion. In
fact, once she aligned herself with Carla and Marie, she changed her expressed
view completely. Where the discussion focused primarily on a rejection of the
text and author, Lynette revealed her ability to consider both the content of
the text and its potential power to address injustice. Although it is encourag-
ing that Lynette linked the text directly to local power issues in the school,

her response also issues a critical call to educators to consider the urgency of addressing students' learning contexts as an integral step in efforts to teach for social justice. Her observation that "I see it every day happen to kids and they don't do anything about it" calls into question the true impact of socially just pedagogy in contexts where fundamental power inequities go unchallenged and unchanged in students' daily life in school.

REENVISIONING SOCIALLY JUST READING IN THE CLASSROOM

The problems of classroom practice I've illustrated in this chapter may be seen in any classroom, but may look different depending on the context. In other classrooms, students may focus more on other aspects of identity such as gender or class, and alliances may form around a different set of ideas. Some of the challenges to socially just teaching and to critical reading, however, may look the same. Figure 5.5 reflects how problems of practice can serve as a starting point for reenvisioning how students' classroom reading might create opportunities for transformative learning. In Chapter 6, we will consider different strategies for responding to the situations outlined in this chapter as a starting point for seeing ways forward for teaching and learning.

Figure 5.5. Shifting Classroom Reading Toward a Vision for Socially Just Learning

FROM	TO
Some students silenced or positioned negatively on the basis of identity	All students have voice
Some ideas silenced or unvoiced	All ideas openly and respectfully considered The class continually reflects on and explores: What does this help us understand about social justice? What are the implications?
Disagreement	Exploration
Reading to fit an existing schema	Reading to revise and develop one's ideas about life, the world, oneself, and others
Reading that forecloses possibilities —OR— Hegemonic reading—group meaning making that reinforces naturalized ideas about inequality and difference	Reading that imagines new possibilities and ways of being, thinking, and believing

CHAPTER SIX

Practicing the Art of Socially Just Teaching

Strategies for Everyday Classroom Use

HOW ISSUES OF SOCIAL justice matter in students' lives and what grounds this provides for socially just teaching can be discovered through continually listening to students to develop our understanding of the words and worlds from which they come. Socially just teaching should attend to the human needs of students as well as to the sociopolitical contexts and purposes for their learning. This can be deeply personal work, as we saw in Chapters 4 and 5.

Melissa, like many other English language arts teachers, used texts as a means to "teach social justice"—to create empathy, understanding, and a shared sense of responsibility for racial hierarchies and oppressive social dynamics. Yet the use and reading of these texts at times created the possibility for students—both White and African American—to reassert problematic racial Discourses and positions that could serve to perpetuate racially divisive ideas and practices. Students' focus on racial injustice as an individual—rather than social—problem ultimately supported the status quo. As Lankshear and McLaren (1993) note, this position can enable students to sidestep collective participation in social transformation, a result that fundamentally undermines the potential for constructive social change.

But to what extent can educators expect students to analyze racism or other conditions of injustice when they are only 15 years old and their primary experiences of racial identity and racism may be largely interpersonal, forged in segregated and strained relationships within their local school and community? How do we imagine a way forward for Melissa and her students?

Throughout this chapter, I will consider how repositioning reading, readers, texts, and contexts in instruction might enable critical readings and socially just possibilities in the classroom. Within each section, we will examine strategies for working with students' responses to text that can help teachers navigate the complex realities of enacting socially just pedagogy.

RESPONDING TO CRITICAL MOMENTS
IN CLASSROOM READING

Chapter 5 focused on observing and analyzing students' discourse and inter-actions to make sense of problems of practice that can arise during reading events. When alignments and alliances occurred along the lines of racial and gender identity, these critical moments created opportunities for Melissa to help students engage in higher levels of social and textual analysis. Yet al-though Melissa worked consistently to enact socially just pedagogy, critical moments sometimes created perplexing challenges for response. She at times expressed frustration at knowing "where to go" when responding to students' meanings and interactions as they unfolded in the classroom.

In this chapter, we will examine several pedagogical approaches and re-lated strategies that can help teachers like Melissa reenvision classroom read-ing. These are

- repositioning the act of reading;
- repositioning the identities of readers; and
- reading and responding to race and identities in context.

To illustrate how these approaches can work, we will revisit and reenvision critical moments from Melissa's class that were explored in depth in Chapter 5. While critical moments are specific to particular readers, texts, and contexts and to some extent defy preconceived responses, I offer these possibilities and strategies as a means to inform our efforts to help students read for social justice—and in socially just ways.

The First Approach: Repositioning Reading and Shifting Our Stance

In making sense of critical moments in the classroom, we can consider how reading was enacted and positioned and what difference this may have had on the opportunities students had for meaning making. Hammerberg (2004) reminds us that "the literacy activities and lessons that we provide in the classroom encapsulate our views of comprehension—whether we see it as residing in the print and the student's cognitive abilities, or whether we see it as being more socially and culturally situated—and this has vast implications in terms of the value placed on diverse knowledges and experiences" (p. 655). One way to analyze and reimagine critical moments, then, is to consider what kind of reading paradigm is reflected within a particular literacy activity and how this may have constrained students' opportunities for considering and valuing diverse experiences, meanings, and ways of reading.

The critical sociocultural model of reading outlined in Figure 6.1 draws from transactional, interactional, critical, and sociocultural understandings of the reading process. Reading is not a standardized act, but rather a complex process of meaning making involving interactions and transactions among situated reader(s), texts, and contexts (Anderson & Pearson, 1984; Gee, 2001; Moje, Dillon, & O'Brien, 2000; Rosenblatt, 1993, 2004; Rumelhart, 1994). Readers do not have solitary relationships with the texts they read; rather, they engage with particular texts in situated contexts. The interactions among reader, text, and context therefore shape how readers make meaning and what meanings are made. Figure 6.1 shows how power and meaning making occur in the interactions and transactions between readers, texts, and contexts such that each element shapes and is shaped by the others during classroom reading. This suggests that the focus of instruction during reading events should be neither exclusively on the reader nor on the text, but on what happens between and among readers, texts, and contexts.

Figure 6.1. A Critical Sociocultural Model of Reading

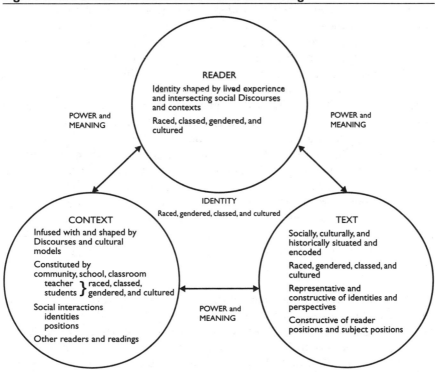

When reading is approached as primarily a relationship between readers and texts, the act of reading within diverse classrooms can negatively position readers by focusing too heavily on one of two extremes: (1) too great a focus on the text, or (2) an overemphasis on the (racially and culturally situated) reader. Focusing too much on the text can overemphasize the authority and meanings of particular text and cause the objective of reading to become merely the acquisition of fixed meanings. Overemphasizing the reader, however, can lead to purely subjective readings that are unaccountable to texts or other readers; this can undermine the objectives of a socially just pedagogy if oppressive patterns of meaning making and interaction are unquestioningly reproduced.

The kinds of discourse and interactions that take place in classrooms shape what counts as knowledge (Bourne & Jewett, 2004; Maher & Tetreault, 1997; Rex, 2000, 2001). When teachers and students enact a model of reading that overemphasizes the role of either reader or text, this may then work against the larger goals and premises of socially just pedagogies. On the one hand, students may be constrained by the ideas of the texts that are chosen for class—if they are not taught to think critically about those texts. On the other hand, if students are not accountable to the text itself, meaning making becomes a free-for-all in which students' own meanings prevent them from considering the ideas of others—or from even truly reading the text at all.

In Melissa's classroom, reading was central to critical moments when issues of racial identity and power were engaged. Working with the problems of practice she experienced in her particular classroom, we will consider how the act of reading was positioned in those moments and what kind of reading students did and did not do. Melissa focused her instruction early in the term on teaching students cognitive strategies for reading, an approach advocated in recent years as a means to give students more explicit mental tools for reading comprehension (Keene & Zimmerman, 1997; Schoenbach, et al., 1999). Although students were taught explicitly to question and make connections with texts, too great an emphasis may have been placed on individual responses to reading, legitimating students' personal responses at the expense of attending to the text in ways that might have better supported critical reading. At times the focus on readers' voices may have allowed students to leave the text behind, leading to an uncritical examination of either the power of the text itself or the power implicit in different readings of the text.

Strategy: Positioning reading as collaborative inquiry. One way to reimagine reading events in Melissa's class would be to shift the teacher's stance—and students' stance—toward the work of reading. A socially just paradigm for classroom reading would emphasize an inquiry approach to working with texts—a more tentative relationship to meaning making that could create a position of collaboration for students across diverse identity and reading positions. This could also create a means to model an ethic of collaboration and social responsibility—and might better support students' comprehension. Van den Branden (2000) found that although classroom talk generally enhanced students' literate achievement and reading comprehension, comprehension was most enhanced when students shared a focus on solving particular problems or challenges in a text. Such an approach can both recognize the raced, classed, and gendered positions students may take and help them construct alternatives to those positions. This can then have important implications for the quality of their reading and learning opportunities.

We enact an inquiry approach to reading in the way we frame and use a given text in the classroom. To see how this might work, we will use the class reading and discussion of "Tar Baby" as a context from which to consider how to reframe the act of reading so as to create conditions for students to better engage in socially just learning (see Chapter 5 for the full transcript and analysis).

Melissa began the class discussion of "Tar Baby" by asking students to share (orally) experiences of racial discrimination similar to that described in the text, and she focused explicitly on the African American girls' experiences and responses. This introduction to the text, I believe, contributed to the racial dynamic surrounding it. Given that the text portrays an African American female author who experiences racial victimization, this setup of the text may have created a "victim" position for some readers in the classroom (dark-skinned African American girls in particular) and a "victimizer" position for others (light-skinned African Americans and White readers). Similarly, with any text we choose to use for socially just purposes, we need to consider, What are the identities and positions that the text affords a given reader? What are the potential threats and risks involved in the reading?

In the case of the "Tar Baby" lesson, the subject position created through the text (through the perspective of an African American girl who experienced racial oppression because of the darkness of her skin) was aligned with the racial identities of several readers (African American girls in the classroom). This alignment may have shaped the resistant responses of students like Lynette (AA) and Carla (AA), who were positioned by Melissa (a White teacher) to "make connections" with the text, but who may not have wanted to align with victimized positions, if such position would make them socially vulnerable. This may then have led them argue that racial discrimination "doesn't matter" and to publicly reject the premises of the text (even though Lynette privately agreed with it). After all, their public rejection can also be seen as a means of constructing themselves as social agents rather than social subjects.

Instead of constructing a position of alignment between reader(s) and texts, teachers can frame the reading of the text as an act of collaborative inquiry for all readers in the room. Using the "Tar Baby" example, the introduction to the text might sound like this:

The author of the text "Tar Baby" wants us to consider how dark-skinned African American women continue to experience color prejudice and racial discrimination. Today we'll read and discuss her essay to study the issues she raises—and how she writes about them. This essay may at times make us uncomfortable. But let's first try to understand the writer's argument and experience. Let's begin by identifying the specific racial problems she names and the evidence she gives for those problems. We'll also consider these problems by making connections to our own experience and to the world around us.

Introducing the text and reading activity in this way reframes the act of reading as a collaborative exercise and inquiry and creates a more equitable subject position for learners by making all readers in the room responsible for engaging with the writer's ideas in the text. It might also work to hold the White students accountable for engaging socially with issues of race, rather than choosing to remain silent. Although racial and gender power dynamics can still come into play, creating an equitable reading position is an important first step to ensuring equitable *access to* and *responsibility for* meaning making during reading events. When we frame classroom reading in this way, we want to empower students to speak to discriminating practices and issues without further disempowering them in the classroom.

This approach also emphasizes the teaching of habits for reading and thinking—not just the teaching of content within the text. To do this, the teacher could engage students in a reading process that positions them to do the shared work of identifying the ideas and evidence in the text. As students share their own connections and evidence from experience, the teacher could help the class think flexibly to gather evidence that confirms, disconfirms, or complicates the claims of the text. Where students do not present or share confirming or complicating evidence, the teacher could pose questions and/or offer examples of experiences that challenge students in those areas of thinking. The teacher could also challenge the limits of our experience as a form of evidence. She might ask, for example: *What does our experience help us to know? What can we not know from our own experience?*

She could then shift the discussion to consider not only the problems posed in the content of the text, but also in the ways the text is written. For example, she might ask students to identify places in the text where the author's tone or language may have distracted them (as readers) from the argument, thereby allowing some students to voice their objections to the ways they perceived the text positioning light-skinned African American women. She might even engage students in attempting to revise lines in the text in ways that preserve the author's argument while reenvisioning the tone of the piece. Without detracting from a consideration of the social issue of racism, then, the teacher might enable students to read collaboratively to address two "problems" posed by the text: (1) the issues of racism and sexism addressed in the content and (2) how the writer's argument is written and its effect on readers.

Strategy: Positioning the teacher as co-reader. While the critical sociocultural model of reading (see Figure 6.1) places the teacher within the reading context, the model cannot represent the power of the teacher (or the researcher) in shaping that context, nor can it sufficiently portray the way the teacher's identities (e.g., raced, classed, gendered) interact with the other readers in the classroom. In fact, I debated whether the teacher in particular belonged at the center of the transactions, because the teacher has the power to choose the texts of the classroom, to shape the learning context, and to shape how students' identities as readers might be positioned in the classroom.

The racial identity of the teacher is one significant factor in shaping students' reading opportunities and experiences in the classroom. Many scholars have noted that the way in which White teachers construct race, even within critical or multicultural pedagogy, can serve to marginalize students of color and reify White identities and Whiteness as central (Banning, 1999; Paley, 1979; Pixley & VanDerPloeg, 2000; Sleeter, 2004). Banning (1999), noted, for example, that although the feminist teacher whose classroom she studied positioned herself as a critical pedagogue, her failure to interrogate her own Whiteness undermined her pedagogical intentions in the classroom. Certainly, then, it is not enough to teach students to read critically for race, class, gender, and power unless teachers are willing to do so as well by carefully examining their own identity and power in the classroom.

A White teacher choosing texts for diverse classroom readers implicitly engages in a political act, for she may select texts for multicultural purposes on the basis of her perception of the racial identities and experiences of students and can use them in ways informed by her assumptions about how the text may be taken up and what meanings students are likely to make. It is possible, then, that teachers aiming to enact socially just teaching practice place an undue burden on students for addressing issues of identity and power if they do not explicitly engage their own identities in the learning work as well. To what extent, for example, is the teacher's choice of text and instructional objective a means of further positioning students as raced, gendered, or classed subjects rather than a means for students to experience greater opportunities for identity and meaning making? How might the teacher's role be reimagined to enact more equitable power relationships in the classroom?

In Melissa's classroom, while a social justice agenda was often implicit in the texts students read and the activities they engaged in, her position within that agenda and relative to the students in the classroom was often opaque.

The asymmetry of this power relationship may have contributed to the ways in which students took up the texts Melissa introduced. What I draw attention to here is the politicized nature of the teacher's identity, role, and position in the classroom. Like the identities of other readers and of people portrayed in texts, the identity of the teacher is an important aspect of the interactions that take place around classroom reading. In order to create socially just learning opportunities for diverse readers, then, we must consider the teacher's identity, position, and power relative to her students.

One way of diffusing power in Melissa's classroom would be to make the learning objectives and purpose of the teacher more transparent and to reimagine her role as that of co-inquirer and co-reader with students in ways that acknowledge her own identity and stake in the learning process in which she asked students to engage. When introducing students' study of the text *A Raisin in the Sun*, for example, Melissa engaged students in several discussions and activities designed to frame their reading of the text. She invited students to first write about and discuss their dreams for the future and potential obstacles to those dreams. This led to students' discussion of whether they perceived their dreams as largely within or out of their control. In a follow-up lesson, students then worked in small groups to generate a list of people who "miss out on America's promises." Although both of these activities allowed students to begin exploring issues of social justice, Melissa herself did not explicitly reveal the purpose of those activities with regard to the text they would be reading, nor did she position herself as a co-reader and investigator of issues of social justice. When the play was first introduced to students, Melissa emphasized the genre of the text and said very little about the content or purpose for reading it. This may have left students unsure of how they were being asked to engage with the text—and what kinds of participation and ideas would "count."

Reimagining the same reading event, the teacher might construct a position of transparency by sharing with students why a particular text was chosen and what she wanted students to know and be able to do as readers with the text. She could then position herself as a co-inquirer by sharing with students what she wonders about through the lens of her own identity and how she's reflecting on ideas about race, gender, and culture in the text. For example, as a White teacher, my introduction to the play *A Raisin in the Sun* might sound something like this:

> *Over the next few weeks, we'll be reading the play* A Raisin in the Sun, *by Lorraine Hansberry. The play is about an African American family in Chicago in the 1950s that is trying to get ahead in life and achieve the American Dream—to be in control of their own destinies. We'll be reading*

the play to consider how the American Dream works—who gets it, who doesn't get it, and why it works differently for different people. Why do some people prosper in America, while others struggle to get by? As part of that exploration we'll consider how race works for the characters in this play and we'll reflect on whether and how this connects to our own lives and to life here at Eastman and in the United States.

We'll also share some of the things we're wondering about as we read the play. For example, as I started reading, I thought about the fact that as a White woman I haven't really experienced racial discrimination. One thing I have been wondering about as I read the play is how the characters make sense of their lives and experiences as African Americans and how the challenges they face may be similar or different to my own experience as a White person. I'm also curious about how race affects their American dreams and what I can learn about that. Based on what you know so far about the text, what do you wonder about? What are some questions we might ask as we begin? Take a few minutes to write down your own questions and what you might want to learn more about through our reading of this play.

Following this introduction, the teacher could give students a few moments to write a response to the question. In order to include as many diverse readings and identities as possible, she might consider collecting students' anonymous responses and sharing several with the class; this would allow diverse readings to be heard and entertained by the whole group. Such an approach could create opportunities, then, for the teacher to model taking an inquiry stance, being transparent about the goals for the reading and about her own racial identity. She could also gather information about students' perceptions going into the text.

The teacher provides an important model for how to talk about race as a means to make sense of the word and the world. Reading for social justice entails risk; our modeling, therefore, needs to reflect the risks we ask students to take when they make meaning about issues of social justice. In her study of two classrooms, Sperling (2003) observed that one of the teachers regularly engaged students in issues of racial identity and invited them to share their personal experiences. Sperling noted, however, that this might have placed an undue burden on students of color to use their personal experiences of race and culture in order to participate academically in the classroom. Rather than implicitly placing the responsibility on students (or on one racial group of students) to engage their racial identities in reading and discussion, the teacher might model how to engage in that kind of reading and talk herself and thereby take greater responsibility for the kind of difficult work required of the text and the reading situation.

I would caution, however, that the work of reading race should be approached carefully and should always be informed by the responses of the particular readers and the circumstances of a given classroom. I am not advocating, for example, that teachers need always ask students to read race or require them to do so; in my study of Melissa's class, she often did not ask students to read race because they often brought racialized meanings to their reading without her prompting. Rather, I am suggesting that socially just teachers must decide when and how to engage race explicitly and when to respond to students' identity talk in the process of teaching and learning. In considering how to respond, I advocate a degree of teacher transparency in approaching the reading of social justice issues with students.

Strategy: Shifting the focus to ways of reading. Teachers engaging in socially just practices can also create better conditions for critical reading by shifting their focus to ways of reading rather than emphasizing the acquisition of particular meanings. While we need to attend to the meanings students make in the classroom and the extent to which these meanings help to forward socially just learning, it is equally important to focus on how students arrive at the meanings they construct. Shifting the classroom focus on reading in this way enacts a socially just paradigm that respects students' right to their own meanings while helping them acquire the intellectual tools for critical thinking and analysis.

Blau's (2003) description of the actions and dispositions of highly literate and critical (what he calls "disciplined") readers provides a means to envision other ways of reading for Melissa's students. For the purposes of considering implications from this study, I will focus only on four of the ways of reading that Blau outlines:

- willingness to suspend closure—to entertain problems rather than avoid them;
- willingness to take risks—to offer interpretive hypotheses, to respond honestly, to challenge texts, to challenge normative readings;
- tolerance for ambiguity, paradox, and uncertainty; and
- intellectual generosity and fallibility: willingness to change one's mind, to appreciate alternative visions, and to engage in methodological believing as well as doubting (Elbow, 1986).

(Blau, 2003, pp. 19–20).

The four reading habits and dispositions outlined above were rarely demonstrated in Melissa's class, particularly when students' readings became entrenched in racial or gender identity positions.

For example, students' discussions of racial power and labeling in their reading of "Tar Baby" may have served more to avoid the social problems addressed in the text than to engage them. The issue of the social disempowerment of dark-skinned Black women was negated by several (mostly light-skinned) African American students, who claimed that the text itself was oppressive to light-skinned Black women. These students' responses to the text expressed a kind of power-evasive discourse (Banning, 1999; Fine, Weis, Powell, & Wong, 1997), one characterized by the speakers' efforts to distance themselves from positions of social power. Darius (AA), for example, considered the argument of the text "outrageous" and viewed it largely as the work of an "angry Black girl" who was called names when she was younger. Several lighter-skinned African American students complained that the author's tone toward light-skinned women was too harsh, and this became a means for dismissing the argument of the text entirely. And throughout most of the exchange, the White students largely remained silent, thereby evading alignment with a position of power as well. Thus students' evasion of power, either through silence or by positioning themselves as victims of the text, prevented the class from taking up and examining the racial experience of the writer and the injustices addressed in the text. In fact, it prevented an examination of power itself.

Yet the meanings students made provide a starting point for helping them learn to suspend closure; after all, students do as readers what they know how to do, not what they have not yet learned or been taught. For example, students might have better entertained ideas and meanings in the text if Melissa herself had modeled for them how to read and consider alternative ideas and meanings—how to engage in methodological believing and doubting. In order for students to learn to suspend closure and entertain complex social problems like racism, the teacher would need to show them explicitly how to suspend closure by demonstrating that approach to reading. She could then help students practice reading in that way to develop more disciplined methods and habits of thinking.

As an example of how the teaching strategy could be enacted, we will revisit the "Tar Baby" discussion to consider how the teacher could instruct students to methodologically believe and doubt the text. Although this illustration focuses on the fourth reading strategy outlined by Blau (2003), the following steps could be used to teach students any of the strategies on that list.

Step 1—Share observations of the ways that students are reading the text.

The teacher might say something like "*I am noticing that many of you are rejecting the ideas in this text by disagreeing with the author's position. You have good reasons for your disagreement, and this shows that many of you are using your connections and responses to make sense of the text. But I am also noticing that no one, except Jade, is taking time to discuss and consider the author's perspective or argument in the text."*

Step 2—Introduce another way of reading and state the purpose for learning it.

To continue, the teacher might say, *"One thing that strong readers do is to try and be intentional about the ways they read for and against the ideas in a text. This habit of thinking and reading is important because it helps us to be systematic in our thinking—to consider as many possibilities in a text as we can before we draw conclusions. Because I don't see anyone using this approach right now, I'd like to show you how it works and try it out as we continue to read and think about this text."*

Step 3—Demonstrate how the strategy works with the text under discussion.

The teacher could then think aloud for students how she methodically believed and doubted certain lines or ideas in the text. She might say something like *"To practice this, I'm going to first read the text to try and believe what the author is saying. As I read, I'll be thinking, 'This could be true because. . . .' I will try to consider what the author is saying and what I know that supports it in any way. For now, I'm going to suspend any disbelief so that I can fully consider the writer's ideas. I'll show you how I do this as I read the first paragraph, then we'll try a few paragraphs of the text together. Once we've tried to systematically believe the author and the viewpoint of the text, then we'll read to systematically doubt it."* Melissa could model this thinking process for students first, then engage them in practicing that way of reading with the text.

Certainly, students could respond to these teacher moves and questions by reasserting problematic meanings. But redirecting the focus of instruction to reading and ways of reading can provide a means of not only including diverse voices and ideas but also raising the level of students' thinking. The socially just teacher's focus would be on demonstrating and naming other ways of reading—such as reading to engage in methodological believing—and would give students opportunities to try on other practices that may be outside their current range of experience. Students would therefore be asked to learn approaches to reading but would not be forced into making a particular meaning. In this way, we can move students toward higher levels of proficiency while fostering a deeper understanding of social justice concepts.

Strategy: Responding to hegemonic readings. At times, students' reading practices worked to construct ideas from text that reinforced normative views of social hierarchies and power structures. When this happened, critical readings and alternatives were not explored. During these moments, teachers might employ a strategy of helping students understand the concept of naturalization—and how their meaning making sustains a status quo that inhibits social justice. This strategy could allow teachers to address moments when issues of race and racial identity may be implicitly engaged but not always overtly expressed.

African American students' responses to texts read for Melissa's class suggest that they were engaged in determining the social and personal significance of their racial and gender identities. Darius (AA), for example, asserted both a sense of pride in his racial and cultural identity and a sense of worry over how his identity might be positioned in ways that could constrain his future social and economic opportunities. When Melissa asked students to express whether they thought their dreams were mostly within or outside of their control (a choice they were asked to indicate by standing on different sides of the room), Darius and the other males in the class overwhelmingly chose the "can control" position, while the majority of the females chose the "can't control" position. Darius's take-up of the "control" position contrasted sharply with the response he took earlier in the same class period when he shared the story of his father's struggle to succeed at work—a struggle marked by obstacles he attributed to race. The class discussions and activities may therefore have posed an identity trap for Darius (and other African American students): Although inviting him to express the possibility that his future chances may be shaped by a racially unjust social system, the class activity may have ultimately made it socially undesirable for him to take the "out of control" position, for this would not have afforded him a sense of agency and an alliance with his male peers in the classroom. In this situation, his response may have been a means to align with notions of individualism and self-sufficiency, even when those ideas contradicted aspects of his personal experience.

Why does a Discourse of individualism matter for students' meaning making the classroom? Studies in psychology have found that girls tend to attribute (academic) achievement difficulties to their own abilities and generally demonstrate lower expectations for success (Ryckman & Peckham, 1987). Ryckman and Peckham found, for example, that across content areas in school, girls tended to attribute success to effort more than boys did, whereas boys tended make attributions to ability and luck. Girls were more likely to attribute failure to ability, forming a pattern described as "learned helplessness": the tendency to see failure as outside one's control and a corresponding sense of helplessness regarding one's future goals and potential for success. Although the salience and universality of these gender patterns has been contested (Holschuh, Nist, & Olejnik, 2001), researchers have found that ability and effort are the most common attributions of success and failure (Graham, 1994) and have noted a relationship between students' attributions and their future goals and emotional reactions (Graham, 1994; Weiner, 1985). Forsyth and Mc-Millan (1981), for example, noted that a sense of control was a critical factor of students' attributions of failure in educational settings because students who perceive their failure as outside their control will not expect future success and may therefore feel helpless. Because the majority of the girls (five of seven) in Melissa's class expressed the sense that their futures may be determined by outside forces, this may put them at risk for the "learned helplessness" described in this body of research.

Yet the boys' responses, which reflected a dominant attribution to forces within one's personal control (nine out of ten males chose the "can control" position), may be problematic as well. Oyserman, Gant, and Ager (1995) found that although individualism and notions of the Protestant work ethic contributed to school persistence and attainment for White students, they found that a different set of identity variables were important for African American students in relation to schooling:

> Gendered African American identity schemas that contain three components—sense of community embeddedness, awareness of racism, and individual effort as an African American (including academic and occupational selves)—will increase school persistence and performance. (p. 1220)

The findings from this study echo those of O'Connor's (1997) study, which found that the take-up of individualistic Discourses might potentially be harmful for African American students' educational resilience and attainment—if they do not have opportunities to develop an awareness and strategic knowledge of racism and a sense of collective struggle against it. These studies suggest, then, that critical moments like those in Melissa's classroom require thoughtful and strategic teacher intervention if the goal is to mediate and address issues of equity and discrimination. How students are positioned as readers and learners in the classroom can therefore have implications for their ability to imagine and construct future identities and opportunities.

Melissa noted the male students' take-up of a Discourse of individualism in the discussion of dreams and attempted to challenge their thinking:

> Melissa: So all of you are saying that as long as you work hard, you can get anything you want in this country.
> *[Students make a few equivocal noises.]*
> Darius (AA): I don't know . . . I don't know . . .
> Jade (AA): If you say you can get anything you want if you just work real hard, that's not always true, because, um . . . sometimes you can work

real, real hard, and you'll not always get what you want to get . . .
[~things sometimes get in the way.][1]
(Field notes and audio transcription, April 19, 2005)

Melissa's intervention created room for doubt, enabling students to voice an idea that complicated the collective acceptance of beliefs about meritocracy and individualism.

Thus both Jade's response, which questioned individualistic Discourses, and the other students' responses, which reified them, pose particular problems for addressing issues of justice and school achievement: For Jade, her response risks positioning her as a victim, unable to act against the obstacles that race and gender may present. For the African American male students, a sense of social agency without recognition of the constraints that may be imposed by a racialized social order could potentially set them up to take all the blame for anything they may not achieve as a result of that social order. And for the White students, this positions them to (consciously or unconsciously) benefit from their racial capital while attributing their achievements to merit alone.

The notion of individual agency without social responsibility can obscure the ways in which the educational and social system can subtly work against students' access to equal educational opportunities. The research suggests that to support diverse student learners, educators need to ensure that students experience both a sense of individual agency *and* an awareness of the ways in which individuals' identities and opportunities may be socially structured and constrained. Further, I would add that students also need various tools to address and work against the social structures that constrain them. How might teachers' responses to critical moments provide these tools and opportunities?

As part of a strategic focus on race and social justice, Melissa could emphasize several important concepts to help students make sense of—and transform—oppressive contexts and practices:

1. Categories of difference are socially and historically constructed as a means for certain groups to acquire power and resources relative to other groups;
2. Racial, class, gender, and cultural identities and meanings are not fixed, but do take shape (and have social consequences) within different contexts; and
3. People can individually and collectively employ strategies to work against oppressive contexts and meanings.

The teacher could address these concepts explicitly with students and provide opportunities for inquiry.

One way to do this might be to teach students how the concept of the "Great Chain of Being" was applied in the late 1800s as a rationale for the economic and social domination of the White racial group over non-White groups. This concept, which hierarchically categorized all forms of life and specifically ordered relationships of subordination among racially designated groups of people, widely influenced scientific and popular thinking and enabled White people to maintain control of social and economic resources and capital (for a detailed overview and analysis of the history of racial categorization, see Lesko, 2001). Along the same lines, students might examine the persistence of institutionalized racism by studying historical texts such as immigration laws. Those instituted in the United States in the early 1900s, for example, worked to exclude certain racial and ethnic groups for fear of social "contamination." Through reading and discussion of these texts, students could come to understand how racial designations are socially constructed to afford power and social capital to some groups at the expense of others. It could also help White students like Dan, Scott, and Sparky to better understand the historical and pervasive roots of racism and its social and material consequences. This approach might also work against the White students' tendencies to equalize their experiences with those of students from other racial backgrounds.

Because a goal of this instructional approach is to teach students strategies for addressing racialized power relations, the teacher might then draw students' attention to what could be done to transform those relations. She might draw students' attention to the characters of Walter and Mama (from *Raisin*), for example, to consider how they defied the White neighborhood association in order to achieve their dream of owning a home. To take this a step further, the teacher could make strategies for social justice the focus of classroom reading and inquiry, providing students with texts (historical and fictional) that illustrate how people worked together to address racial injustice and oppression. She could select texts that showed African American and White people working together, thereby providing student readers with subject positions other than those of victim and victimizer. Such an approach could provide powerful models for students to envision socially just contexts, communities, and identities—and the strategies needed to achieve them.

The Second Approach: (Re)situating the Identity of the Reader— "Why They Have to Talk Like We All One People?"

Edward's question, raised during a class discussion of the play *A Raisin in the Sun* by Lorraine Hansberry, suggests that when readers' racial identities align with the racial identities portrayed in texts, teachers need to attend carefully to students' responses to understand what sense they are making of racial identity via their reading. Addressing identity issues in reading involves recognizing that students have the right to choose their identities, as well as their ideas; it also requires that teachers acknowledge students' expressions of their identities, even when those expressions pose conflicts or challenges to the instruction at hand.

Across the data from my research in Melissa's class, African American students were more likely to take up issues of racial identity in texts and White students were more likely to silence them, a finding consistent with other research (Maher & Tetreault, 1997; Pixley & VanDerPloeg, 2000). Given the significance of this pattern in students' meaning making, it is important to give voice to issues of racial identity rather than glossing over the very issues that matter to students themselves.

The act of recognizing students' expressed identities reflects a basic tenet of culturally relevant instruction (Hammerberg, 2004; Ladson-Billings, 2000). It is also a first step in helping student readers learn how identities are shaped by texts and Discourses and how to develop the strategic knowledge to resist or refigure those Discourses (Mellor & Patterson, 2000). Responding to critical moments requires taking up issues of identity in reading, a strategy we will explore in the next section.

Strategy: Taking up identities in reading. In Melissa's class, students at times explicitly engaged issues of race and racial identity in their reading across multiple texts. In other contexts, we may see students draw on other aspects of identity that figure powerfully in their lives: class, gender, physical ability, or sexuality, for example. When this occurs, it is important that teachers acknowledge and build upon students' responses to create equitable classroom contexts and meaning-making opportunities during classroom reading events. This requires that teachers listen for—and take up—students' identity talk.

When Edward (AA) responded to the text by asking, "Why they have to talk like we all one people?" he initiated a critical moment, bringing issues of racial identity and power to the reading of *Raisin*. In this situation, Melissa did not take up the issue he addressed. However, we can consider how the teacher might respond in a way that could both reposition the act of reading and Edward as a (raced and gendered) reader. In order to recognize his identity and experience as a reader and to clarify his comment, we might begin by saying, *"Edward, I'm interested in how you're responding to the text right now. Can you explain what you mean?"*

Follow-up questions might then build on the issues of racial identity that Edward raised: *"What lines in the text raise this question for you? Are you questioning Walter, the character, or Lorraine Hansberry, the author?"* This move invites students to question and explore the racial representations in the text by first acknowledging how (and where) Edward perceived the text as positioning racial identities.

The teacher could then help students examine how texts create identities and why Lorraine Hansberry may have chosen to have Walter talk as though African Americans were "all one people." The following passage provides an opportunity for such inquiry:

> Walter: That is just what's wrong with the colored woman in this world . . .
> don't understand about building their men up and making 'em feel like they
> somebody. Like they can do something. (Hansberry, 1988, p. 34)

The teacher would need to demonstrate how to read and recognize the racial and gender identity construction in phrases such as "the colored woman." She could then invite Edward and the rest of the class to do a similar analysis with another line from the text. As students continue to read the play, they could find examples of identity talk by and about various characters as a means to study how characters position one another in relation to their socially perceived identities. To help students consider how literature gives us a means to develop insight into issues of social power and position, the teacher could also lead students to an understanding of how we might understand the purpose of the text and of the author's use of characterization to illuminate challenging ideas.

All this analysis would lead, ideally, to a greater understanding of how individuals can have differential access to power according to their socially constructed identities. For example, the teacher could help students question the identities and social realities in the text by asking some of the following questions:

1. How does Walter think about himself as an African American?
2. How does Walter's identity as African American influence the way other characters such as Beneatha (AA) or Lindner (W) view him?
3. How does Walter's racial identity shape his dreams? What can he—and can't he—control?
4. Why do you think Lorraine Hansberry (the author) draws our attention to race in this way?

Using the text itself, students could then consider how characters' contexts and circumstances shape their actions and opportunities. Using race and gender as lenses for analysis, the class could consider the following questions:

1. How does a given character's racial or gender identity work to his or her advantage or disadvantage in a certain social context?
2. How does a given character's race or gender shape who he or she is in the context of the story—and who he or she is allowed to be or become?

3. How might it be otherwise? What else might this character have said or done? How could the social context change to become more just?

By engaging in this process, students could learn how identity (and racial and gender identity in particular) is not fixed or predetermined, but socially recognized and constructed. Asking students to imagine other possibilities for characters' identities and social contexts could also help them develop discursive strategies for social and personal transformation. While this case focused on racial and gender identity aspects, the broader idea here is to provide students with specific lenses for making sense of identity in context—according to what aspects of identity matter most in context and in students' talk.

Sleeter and Bernal (2004) note that although the insights of critical pedagogy and their implications are valuable, the power to name social justice issues and how they are addressed has important implications the valuing or devaluing of students' identities and cultures. The critical tradition of deconstructing notions of culture and identity can certainly run the risk of violating the very racial, ethnic, and cultural identities that some students and communities hold sacred. How students are invited to share and explore their racial and cultural identities—and to what end—therefore matters enormously for enacting a socially just teaching practice. While teachers can help students to question the ways in which racial and cultural identities are socially and discursively constructed, they must ultimately create the means to protect those identities by respecting what they mean to students themselves.

The Third Approach: Creating Contexts for Reading That Support Diverse Readers

Rather than focusing on abstract notions of justice and identity, socially just pedagogy should address the contexts of students' everyday lives to transform persistent discourses that sustain unjust notions of difference and power. In advocating that teachers address "commonsense sexism and racism," Ng (1995, p. 129) points out, however, that efforts to "teach against the grain" are often met with student resistance. As we saw in Melissa's classroom, resistance can come from unlikely places, for even as Melissa sought to address issues of racial identity and power, students who did not benefit from the status quo nevertheless acted publicly to maintain it. Much of the difficulty came in when students were asked to share ideas in whole-group discussion. This context for reading—inside the larger contexts of the school and community—may have figured largely in shaping the kinds of reading and responding students did. The following section thus considers how teachers can construct and respond to local contexts for reading in order to create conditions that support the inclusion and consideration of diverse perspectives.

Strategy: Teaching students to read context. While it is important that teachers structure supportive classroom contexts, if we hope to help students become reflective, socially responsible citizens, we must teach them to read their own contexts with the lens of social justice. Socially just educators can help students become more aware of their social contexts, reflect on those contexts, and work to reshape them—to read not only the word, as Freire (1994) says, but the world as well.

Returning to the data and to the challenges Melissa faced, one strategy would be to juxtapose the reading of text with the reading of context, to help students not only name school segregation as a problematic social practice but also treat this aspect of context as a focus for inquiry and problem solving. Take, for example, the instance of students' raced and gendered responses to *Raisin* that were illustrated in Chapter 5. When the students began to form raced and gendered alliances in the debate about the power dynamic between Walter and Ruth, a possible teacher response might have sounded like this:

> *I'm going to stop us for a moment and share some of the things I am noticing. First, I see that several of you feel very strongly about these characters. This is important because it shows that we're thinking carefully about the characters' experiences and motivations, and that we're analyzing those aspects of the play. I'm also noticing that the boys seem to be siding with Walter and the girls seem to be siding with Ruth, and that the White students in the classroom haven't said anything yet, so I'm wondering why these patterns are happening. Let's take a moment to reflect on that in writing, and then we'll discuss our thinking about that.*

By pausing the discussion in this way, the teacher can model critical questioning to interrogate how students' alignments and social practices around reading are naturalized. The class might even engage in partner and whole-group discussion to name how social segregation "works" at school, whom it benefits and how, and what steps could be taken (and by whom) to transform the classroom and school context.

Although it is certainly possible that students' responses could further complicate the discussion and serve to confound rather than improve efforts to engage in critical analysis, teaching students to explicitly and routinely read contexts and reflect on their own meaning-making practices nevertheless provides them with opportunities to become metacognitive about the sociocultural nature of their reading. Perhaps more important, it could give students a role in the hard work of reshaping their social contexts by providing opportunities to engage in different ways of talking and behaving.

While noting that my focus thus far has been on the use of traditional print texts in the classroom, teachers could also use transcripts of student talk to help them examine how identities are constructed and positioned through classroom conversation. In other words, transcripts of students' discussions could themselves become the text they read in order to analyze their own reading context. In my work with case study readers for this research, for example, I asked students to examine classroom transcripts and to make observations about their own and others' talk. This provided students with opportunities for reflection on the nature of students' interactions and how these shaped the meanings that were made. Teachers might therefore consider using short transcripts of classroom discourse to illustrate and complicate students' ideas as they are represented in students' everyday talk in school. This can also help develop students' awareness of their uses of language and the Discourses they may perpetuate.

Teaching students how language works to construct identities can help to transform the reading context. We could, for example, link students' reading of texts and contexts by asking students to examine and reflect on a transcript of the "Tar Baby" discussion. This would create the opportunity to challenge students' assertion that race "doesn't matter" and that nothing can be done about racial injustice. We might, for example, ask students to reexamine Bob's (AA) argument that the kind of race and color talk that happened at Eastman was "just blazin'"—a kind of casual banter or teasing. As a means for analysis, students could generate criteria for when race talk does and doesn't matter. We could then help students use the criteria to co-construct written guidelines for their talk and actions in the classroom so that students' racial and gender identities could better be respected. In this way, teachers might be able to help students read—and transform—their context for reading and learning.

CLOSING THOUGHTS

The work of socially just teaching is adaptive—it requires continual engagement with and response to students as readers, thinkers, and members of a literate community. In this chapter, we've examined how social justice might be enacted and explored through students' responses to text and how reading matters in a pedagogy that supports and sustains diverse ways of thinking and being. In the next chapter, we'll look at how we might organize instruction to help students read for social justice within a larger framework or unit of study.

CHAPTER SEVEN

Putting It All Together
Developing a Unit of Study for Social Justice

LEST THE SUBTITLE OF this chapter be deceiving, let me first say that the work of socially just teaching is ongoing and belongs in our everyday practice, not just in a unit of study. As we saw in Chapters 5 and 6, classroom reading and interactions provide important grounds from which to identify ongoing areas of study and help students wrestle with ideas of inclusion, justice, and power in their lives and learning. The story of Melissa's class, though, reflects the importance of being transparent and explicit in engaging students in socially just learning. In a unit of study on social justice, we consider more specifically what we want students to know and be able to do as readers, writers, and thinkers who can engage critically in studying social problems and ideas that sustain inequitable and oppressive conditions.

Rather than approaching social justice through content (e.g., studying workers' rights or a particular historical situation), the approach outlined here focuses on helping students to develop skills and habits of reading for social justice. This curricular framework is designed to help students read for themes related to social justice (e.g., inclusion, difference, power) and can be used with a variety of texts and topics. In the language arts classroom, learning to read for social justice entails the work of analyzing and interpreting language as a medium not only through which issues of justice take form but also through which we can experience the power of literature to provoke us to discovery, empathy, and action. To construct a vision of what this work can look like in practice, I will first describe the framework for a unit focused specifically on reading for social justice. We will then examine a model of the unit in action in Alissa Niemi Heikkila's high school classroom.

WHAT STUDENTS NEED TO KNOW AND BE ABLE TO DO TO READ, WRITE, AND THINK IN SOCIALLY JUST WAYS

In Chapter 4, we considered how the work of reading with personal inquiry can help students develop habits of thinking that support engaged and purposeful learning. Building on that approach, this unit helps students to use a similar reading process with specific lenses that help them understand and analyze concepts, conditions, and situations related to social justice. In other words, the unit allows instruction to explicitly teach students what to do in their reading to help them recognize and make sense of these ideas. Students learn to reflect on these concepts and their implications in reading in ways that support a stance of ongoing inquiry into how the social world works and how things might be otherwise.

Figure 7.1 outlines what we want students to know and be able to do when reading with a socially just lens. While the Common Core Standards, for example, emphasize the importance of learning to read critically, the purpose of the critical reading work in this unit is to consider the implications of texts and ideas for the interests of marginalized and socially vulnerable people. It also asks students to imagine alternatives to existing social realities in order to develop what North (2009) calls a "visionary literacy."

LENSES FOR SOCIALLY JUST READING

If we want students to learn to do the critical reading work outlined above, we need to name and demonstrate the *what* and *how* of that work. In considering the goals and design of a unit focused explicitly on social justice, then,

Figure 7.1. Student Outcomes for a Unit on Reading for Social Justice

What Students Need to Know	What Students Need to Be Able to Do
Social worlds are built on systems and ways of interacting that we may think of as "natural," but which in fact are constructed by people for different purposes	Read texts using lenses for social justice to identify and analyze how concepts like power play out in human interactions and institutions—and to what effects
Societies are organized in ways that confer power and privilege to some groups over others	Critically question the ideologies and actions that contribute to social injustices
How power and privilege are conferred, and what resources are available to which groups, are matters of equity and justice	Make sense of what concepts like marginalization, oppression, and power actually mean in the lives and opportunities of individuals and groups
Groups are often defined in terms of identities based on socially constructed ideas about things like race, class, culture, gender, sexuality, physical ability, and the like	Imagine alternatives to social conditions, individual actions, and social and political structures

we begin by defining the lenses critical readers use to guide their habits of thinking in a social justice paradigm. Bomer and Bomer (2001) outline several important concepts that critical readers need to understand in order to engage in social critique, reflection, and action. We can use these guiding concepts as lenses for inquiry with the texts students read. The explicit naming of these lenses provides essential scaffolding for all other learning in the unit. I detail several of these briefly here, and will revisit them as we consider how students can apply these lenses to their reading work.

Power. Critical readers concerned with social justice examine who has power, how it is acquired, and how it is used to empower or oppress others. Power may be thought of as institutional as well as interrelational. Relationships of power create and sustain the social conditions that structure access to social resources and opportunities. Reading literary texts gives students opportunities to consider how individuals' lives are shaped and constrained by the power (or lack thereof) afforded to them through their position in the larger social structure. It also provides a context for students to imagine how power might be redistributed more justly and for the greater social good.

Identities and Social Positions. We can think of society as composed of different groups with which people align themselves or to which they are considered to "belong." Critical readers consider how groups are constructed and defined through language, how the identities of group members are positioned in social contexts, and how members of different groups may be privileged or marginalized. When making sense of issues of social justice, we consider which groups have a stake in a given situation and how those groups are positioned relative to one another. For example, students may consider how the rights, interests, and identities of Native American groups are legally positioned relative to the U.S. government or to mainstream White society.

Representation. Critical readers notice that how individuals and groups are portrayed through language can act to advantage—or disadvantage— members of different groups. Sometimes we may notice that a text does not represent a given group or perspective at all; at other times, we can detect a creeping sense of interpretation that colors how we are asked to make sense of the identities, motives, and credibility of a certain group of people. Whether reading literary or nonfiction texts, we consider who portrays whom, for what purpose, and to what possible advantage.

Naturalization. The concept of naturalization draws our attention to aspects of our social world that we take for granted or that seem or are assumed to be "normal." There is a common belief, for example, that if you work hard, you will succeed in America. Yet when I drive through many urban areas, there are clearly sections of great wealth and poverty. We can see these social and economic disparities and think that those who struggle, those who have less, just don't work as hard as their wealthy neighbors. We might think, "That's just the way things are." Using the concept of naturalization helps us to consider, how else might things be? How does what appears "natural" arise from human choices and actions, and who benefits from the notion that this is "just the way things are?"

Justice. Justice relates to notions of equity, as discussed in Chapter 1. Considerations of justice, however, go beyond what is "fair" to thinking about what actions are morally right and how people might live among each other in ways that allow them to live peacefully and have their human needs and rights met. Using the lens of justice, we consider texts and situations from a stance that seeks to protect and care for the socially vulnerable and to continually envision how the social world can be better for all people.

Voice/Multiple Perspectives. When reading with the lens of social justice, we consider whose voices in a given political or social situation might be marginalized or underrepresented. We try to make sense of unjust conditions and situations through a consideration of the multiple parties who have a stake, and whose realities may or may not be well represented in a given conflict. We look at the larger human impact of a given injustice and listen for the ways in which people's voices and experiences can point us toward understandings and solutions that uphold human dignity and fairness.

Money, Wealth, and Poverty. Because the distribution of money and resources in society constitutes a fundamental justice issue, critical readers notice aspects of texts that help us understand how inequities in wealth are created and sustained and how poverty develops as a form of oppression. Understanding economic disparities as socially constructed rather than naturalized allows us to consider how political and social structures might better ensure just living conditions for all people.

Violence and Peace. When we inquire into the causes of violence and the means to sustain peace, we can read in ways that focus our attention on the social conditions that contribute to violence and the processes necessary to diffuse it. Reading stories of war and human rights abuses, for example, cannot offer the possibility of social transformation without the tools for analyzing conflict and how alternatives to violence can be created.

As with the reading work on personal inquiry outlined in Chapter 4, the instruction in this unit engages students in a reading process that cultivates an exploratory stance toward texts and ideas, asking students to try on ways of reading rather than calling for them to acquire particular meanings. In so doing, we seek to create a socially just process for learning that provokes critical thought while leaving room for students to construct their own meanings.

Furthermore, the concepts defined above do not exist in isolation and are not mutually exclusive. We can help students think about how each concept relates to others to consider, for example, how different groups use power to control which voices are heard and which are silenced. Without explicit instruction and practice in using these lenses, we risk asking students to engage in thinking work that remains opaque; this can cause frustration if students don't know what, specifically, they are being asked to do. This approach also prevents us from creating a context in which students try to arrive at "our" meanings—rather than using critical tools for constructing their own. At the heart of this thinking work is the understanding that social worlds are made, not fixed; that they can be changed; and that reading is part of a transformative process.

A SAMPLE OUTLINE OF AN INQUIRY UNIT ON SOCIAL JUSTICE

We can think of the unit in terms of three phases. In each phase, students' roles shift toward increasing independence and application of the thinking and reading work of the unit. Concepts for social justice are introduced in the first phase of study as students learn to consider these concepts as part of their work with selected texts they read together. As the unit progresses, students apply the concepts to their own reading in independent texts or small groups reading the same text. Figure 7.2 outlines what the first phase entails.

Phase 1: Introducing Lenses and Ways of Reading

The first phase of instruction focuses on introducing the lenses for social justice and how to use them for reading. Each lens should be explicitly introduced, explained, and modeled for students in the context of meaningful reading. The first phase of instruction uses the direct instruction, modeling, and guided practice stages of gradual release to prepare students for working independently with the lenses in the context of reading their own novels in Phase 2.

When Alissa launched the social justice unit with her students, she used a reading workshop structure to organize shared instruction and independent learning in ways that supported students' agency and access to texts with

Figure 7.2. Reading for Social Justice Unit, Phase 1:
Introducing Lenses and Ways of Reading

What Mini-Lessons Focus On	What Students Are Doing as Independent Readers
Introducing and providing guided practice in using lenses for socially just reading Trying on the reading work with shorter, shared texts Exploring and refining concepts through discussion	Trying on lenses for reading with guided support (using a shared class text) Developing an inquiry stance toward exploring ideas of social justice in texts Taking text-based notes on examples of social justice concepts and questions

which they could meaningfully explore the concepts. For whole-group work and guided practice, she chose to read excerpts from *The Absolutely True Diary of a Part-Time Indian,* by Sherman Alexie (2007), and provided modeling and guided practice in analyzing the text using the lenses for social justice. In the novel, the main character, Junior (also known as Arnold), describes his life in poverty on the Spokane Indian Reservation and his experience of leaving his community to attend and all-White school. Alissa chose the text to help students explore the concepts of poverty, opportunity, and racial identity and oppression.

As she introduced, modeled, and coached students in using each lens, Alissa used the "Reading for Social Justice" tool presented in Figure 7.3 as a means to help habits of mind take shape in students' reading and interactions with texts. The tool served to anchor students' reading work across the unit as they developed questions and theories about themes of social justice with the passages they read together from Alexie's novel.

Students began using the lenses to guide their work with the text, and the class gathered examples of how each lens helped them think about their reading. Alissa charted these so students could have models of the kind of analysis they would need to do when they began independent reading work in Phase 2. As one example, notice how Bailey, a 9th-grader, used the lens of power to make meaning of a scene from *The Absolutely True Diary* when she described the main character Arnold's experience in one scene from the novel:

> Arnold ended up in an all-white school, (mind you, he is from an Indian reservation) when he was in geology and his (white) teacher was explaining how wood becomes petrified wood. Arnold raised his hand and explained how petrified wood really isn't wood once it has become petrified. His teacher Mr. P got extremely upset at Arnold for contradicting his teachings, but when Gordy (another white kid) raised his hand and explained that Arnold was correct, Mr. P gave Gordy all

Figure 7.3. Reading for Social Justice

Concepts Related to Social Justice	Things to Notice	Questions We Can Ask	Examples from My Book
Power	How the social world is organized (e.g., how hierarchies are organized, how political power is distributed) How characters interact with one another Who does/does not have power to do what	How do certain groups or individuals become powerful? How is power expressed and what are the effects (for the powerful and for those who do not have power)?	
Identities and Social Positions	How characters think about and position themselves and others as members of certain groups with a particular social identity (e.g., based on race, ethnicity, class, gender, or sexuality) How members of certain groups are treated and whether that treatment is just How social positions influence the power and opportunities afforded to different people	How do ideas about group membership or identity shape the ways people see themselves and how they interact with one another? How do identities and social positions shape one's opportunities?	
Representation (How People Are Portrayed)	How characters in the text portray (describe or talk about) each other as particular "kinds of people" or members of groups How the author portrays characters as particular "kinds of people" or members of groups	How does the way in which characters are portrayed contribute to or complicate stereotypes of groups to which those characters belong? How does the way in which characters are portrayed shape the ways they see themselves or the ways that others see them?	
Naturalization (Taking for Granted the Way the World "Works")	What actions, ways of interacting, or situations characters in the world of the story consider "normal" How characters' perceptions of what is "normal" shape their ways of acting and interacting	What assumptions do characters make about "how things are" or how they "are supposed to be"? How do the things characters take for granted (things that are naturalized) work to the advantage or disadvantage of some people or groups? How might the social world of the story be different?	

Justice	What opportunities characters do/do not have What social rules or laws allow people to do/not do certain things and why Situations that are unfair or that favor one person or group over another	What choices do characters have about their lives? Do all of the characters have equal opportunities or access to equal opportunities? What prevents characters from having equal opportunities, and how might things be different?
Voice/Multiple Perspectives	Who gets to speak and who does not Who has the power to control what voices are heard or silenced What perspectives are represented and what perspectives are silenced or underrepresented (either by the author or within the story itself)	How do the voices represented in the text shape the story that is told? If other voices or perspectives were included, how might this change the characters' ways of acting or thinking? How might it change the story or our understanding of it?
Money, Wealth, and Poverty	Who has/does not have money and what difference this makes for characters' opportunities or chances in life How characters or groups use money to advance their own interests	What does money buy or not buy in this text? How is money connected to power or privilege in this story? How does it create situations that unfairly advantage or disadvantage certain groups?
Violence and Peace	How characters solve problems What causes characters to behave violently toward one another The consequences of violence How characters respond in the face of violence What choices characters have as alternatives to violence	What alternatives do characters have when faced with violent situations or choices? What are the causes (personal, social, economic, or political) of violence (i.e., war) and what could prevent or alter those causes? What does it mean to work for peace?

the credit for figuring out the petrified wood story! I think this shows
POWER that Mr. P has over Arnold. I noticed that Mr. P only listened to
Gordy because he was white. (Written response)

Students' work with the lenses showed them approximating their use of
the concepts, given their newly acquired understanding, as we see in Bailey's
response. Because the class engaged in literary discussion designed to help
them explore their thinking for this purpose, Alissa was able to use partner,
small-group, and whole-class discussions to deepen students' understanding and analysis. When she noticed that students' responses shut down critical thought and perpetuated troubling Discourses (as we saw in Melissa's
classroom in Chapter 5), Alissa found opportunities for teachable moments
through which she could "disturb" their understandings.

Alexie's novel offers important opportunities for students to understand
the main character's experience of poverty and racial alienation as a Native
American growing up on a reservation in the state of Washington. However,
Alissa's students at times struggled to use the text as a starting point for inquiry rather than as a basis for passing judgments. Consider, for example, the
following excerpt from a small-group discussion following the reading of an
early chapter in the book. Here we see a small group of students working to
explore ideas in the text following Alissa's mini-lesson on how to use lenses
when reading:

Student 1: I was kind of confused, like when he says that his dad gets
    drunk and his dad buys all the books, it may be like his parents waste
    all their money on like their old dreams; like his mom still wants to
    be a teacher . . . and his dad drinks away his pain or something? I
    thought that was kind of . . . like . . . so they don't have any money
    for food, but it's like cheap, so they buy books and alcohol, but they
    should be using the money to buy food.
Student 2: I think it's kind of preventing them from really seeing
    their dreams because I don't think people are just like prevented
    from doing their dreams. If somebody stops them, if they are really
    motivated, then they would be able to.
Student 3: Yeah.
Student 4: I don't think anyone's stopping them. I just think that they
    see everyone else like their friends' parents and they just believe that
    they can't do it so they don't even try.
Student 1: That goes back to what he says like how people . . . his
    parents are poor and they come from a poor family . . . they came
    from poor people and so on, so do they all just think they are
    destined to be poor? (Transcript of small-group discussion)

This example of small-group discussion shows how students' responses at times reinforced stereotypes of lower-income and Native people as lazy and undisciplined, a phenomenon I analyzed in depth in Chapters 5 and 6. Rather than suspending judgment and using the text to explore the limits of their understandings about poverty, the students in this group (and others) evoked a "bootstraps" Discourse to draw conclusions about why the characters have not overcome poverty to just "do their dreams." As Alissa and I monitored students' discussions and gathered examples of their ideas, we discussed how we might disrupt their thinking to open up other ways of exploring the text to consider how poverty structures opportunities. We also wanted them to shift to an inquiry stance in order to question the limits of individual agency in overcoming oppressive circumstances.

On the following day, Alissa used the preceding discussion excerpt to revisit how to read in ways in which we resist our assumptions and take on different points of view. The class examined the transcript to practice raising questions and suspending closure (Blau, 2003) as a means to revise and practice their discussion work (for more on this subject, see Chapter 3). These instructional reading moves not only raised the level of students' work with the text but also intentionally helped students to become aware of their assumptions and practice reading to complicate them.

Phase 2: Working with Concepts Independently

Once students had been introduced to lenses for social justice and practiced applying them through shared (whole-class) reading and small-group work, they were ready to take on a greater degree of independence in Phase 2, as described in Figure 7.4.

To set students up for supportive independent work, Alissa gathered sets of multiple texts to which students could apply their work with the reading lenses. While there are many texts to choose from that could work well in this unit, Alissa's reading list included the following:

- *A Long Way Gone: Memoirs of a Boy Soldier*, by Ishmael Beah
- *What Is the What*, by Dave Eggers
- *Sold*, by Patricia McCormick
- *Monster*, by Walter Dean Myers
- *Beloved*, by Toni Morrison

The list of texts includes not only a range of subject matter, but a range of reading levels as well, to give students access to the concepts they were studying through diverse texts. Students chose their texts and were placed in groups of three or four according to their text selection. Group work created a

Figure 7.4. Reading for Social Justice Unit, Phase 2:
Working with Concepts Independently

What Mini-Lessons Focus On	What Students Are Doing as Independent Readers
How to apply a lens to an independent text	Applying lenses for social justice to independently selected texts—either reading alone, in partners, or small groups
How to develop a line of thinking by tracking social justice concepts across a text	
How to develop inquiry that deepens our exploration of a concept about social justice as it plays out in a given text or across multiple texts	Focusing independent writing and discussion on the exploration of particular lenses, according to the purpose of the reader and the opportunities afforded by a given text

context for students to develop their ideas about social justice and their ability to talk about the ideas in the text with depth and specificity.

As students read their books, they noted places in the text that helped them think about a particular lens for social justice. At times, students focused their reading around one particular lens and used their observations to develop a theory about how the text addressed that particular concept of social justice.

To see an example of students' reading work, we can examine some of the notes that one student, Leona, took while she read *Sold*, by Patricia Mc-Cormick (2006). The novel tells the story of Lakshmi, a 13-year-old Nepalese girl who is sold into prostitution to pay her family's debt. As Leona gathered observations from the text, she concluded that the lenses of "money" and "groups" were "sub-categories of power," and that "whoever had money or was in a higher group had more power over everyone." She therefore began to focus her reading primarily around ideas of power in the text.

Figure 7.5 provides an example of Leona's notes. In this entry from her final portfolio, she gathered examples of the adhesive notes she had written throughout the text and which helped her think about power in the characters' lives and circumstances. Her observations of the text helped her make meaning of the relationship between gender, money, and power. This lead her to question how the girls in the brothel respond to their enslavement to prostitution: "I wonder why all of the girls are oppressed but still accept it and embrace whatever they are allowed to have." We can see in Leona's responses not only the work of textual and social analysis but also the seeds of thought from which she might understand and imagine a different world. Her questions helped her to see beyond what has become naturalized for the characters to make sense of the injustices they live through. Her analysis then helped her search for ways that empowerment might be possible for the characters in the social world of the text.

To help students extend their thinking, Alissa modeled how to use notes to write longer responses in their writer's notebooks. Students like Leona might take their observations about the girls' "acceptance" of their exploitation, for example, to pursue a line of thinking about why women in oppressive situations may respond this way, using the reader's experience and evidence from the text. Longer written responses helped students name and elaborate

Figure 7.5. Leona's Responses to *Sold*, by Patricia McCormick, Using the Lens of Power

Sticky Notes—Reading and Thinking for Social Justice—**Sold**
Main Lens—Power

Gender inequality with males as the superior sex	Wealth and money and social class
I wonder if they ever sell a man's belongings in time of need.	I notice that even a teacher has only one pencil and also wonder if it would cost Lakshmi's family more to gamble or just buy 1 single pencil for her.
I infer that men only make any real decisions and stepfather is soon to make one.	I notice how in the past Lakshmi never had her own pencil and now she is very moved just because Harish is giving her a single pencil.
I notice that by not denying the coke, stepfather is in a way acknowledging the fact that Lakshmi was useful.	I notice how Mumtaz is the main controller of money and she is noticeably different from the other females in the household: She's more well fed, doesn't "work," controls how much debt people do or don't owe her and more.
I wonder why all the girls are oppressed but still accept it and embrace whatever they are allowed to have.	
I notice how a man in a way has control over what a woman could look like and wonder why something like hair length can determine how people treat you.	I notice that even though Mumtaz has a lot of money and can bribe the police, they still would do and take whatever they want.
With the introduction of the American man, I wonder how an American woman would be treated.	I wonder how different the city is from the country.
	I wonder how much of a "luxury" tea really is to Lakshmi now that she has to work and save everything.

on their understandings to see what they were thinking. These responses also provided a starting point for small-group discussions and sowed seeds for thought that students developed further in the final phase of study.

Phase 3: Synthesizing and Making a Case

At the end of the unit, students may be asked to synthesize their learning about social justice concepts as they play out in the texts they read independently or in small groups. Having explored ideas of social justice in practice, and having focused continuously on those ideas across their reading of a text, students are then able to pose a thesis about social justice and make a case for their interpretations of social justice concepts as they relate to their reading. Figure 7.6 outlines the instructional work of this phase.

Alissa's students demonstrated their learning through a reading portfolio, in which they reread the notes they took on texts throughout the unit and their extended responses, then reflected on their reading process and how their understanding of social justice concept(s) changed during the course of the unit. Teachers could also choose to have students synthesize their understanding through a longer written piece (e.g., an essay) that demonstrates new theories they developed about social justice and how their theory took shape in the text they read independently.

In part of her portfolio, Leona reflected on how she was able to read for social justice and how this informed her understanding. She wrote:

> In this book I see social injustice through discrimination of women. Girls are sold into prostitution, women have to aid men in many

Figure 7.6. Reading for Social Justice Unit, Phase 3: Synthesizing and Making a Case

What Mini-Lessons Focus On	What Students Are Doing as Independent Readers
How to draw together evidence and thinking from one (long) or multiple (shorter) texts around a given lens	Using adhesive notes and reflections from text(s) to develop and extend their understanding of social justice concepts through their writing
How to explain or elaborate on one's understanding of a concept through written discussion of texts or literature	
How to make a case (argument) using a given lens and evidence from text (might be in the form of an essay, editorial, call to action paper, literary analysis, or proposal)	Synthesizing their ideas and evidence from text to explain a social concept or develop an argument related to social justice

different levels, and older men have way more power. Lakshmi isn't even allowed to look a man in the eye if they aren't related to her. It is socially unjust that women are considered so low in this society and how high and mighty men are even if they are useless and gamble everything away (stepfather).

To describe how her definition of social justice had evolved during the course of the unit, Leona explained:

So far my thinking leans more toward equity than equality. I would rather do what was right than what seems fair to a majority. The hard part is narrowing down the definition of "right."

As we strive to engage students in socially just reading and learning, we too can struggle to define what's "right." Our pedagogical choices, whether expressed through the design of instructional units or in the daily work of classroom teaching, speak to students of how social justice matters both in the content and process of study. Implementing an explicit study in how to read for social justice helps students learn new ways of working with texts and ideas—and for larger social purposes. After all, if students can read the word differently, they are better empowered to read the world differently as well.

CHAPTER EIGHT

Closing Thoughts

Leading for Socially Just Teaching and Learning

> For apart from inquiry, apart from the praxis, individuals cannot be truly human. Knowledge emerges only through invention and re-invention, through the restless, impatient continuing, hopeful inquiry human beings pursue in the world, with the world, and with each other.
>
> —Paolo Freire, *Pedagogy of the Oppressed*, p. 72

I REMEMBER WELL A particular day when I worked with a group of teachers at Heritage High School on the Tulalip Indian Reservation in Marysville, Washington. Like many schools where I have worked, Heritage has many students who struggle academically, who are several years behind grade level in reading, and who will not graduate from high school if they cannot pass the state standardized test. For these students and their teachers, time is running short to ensure that students leave high school prepared to read, write, and think in ways that equip them for life, work, and service to their community—if they stay in school long enough to graduate. "These are the things that keep me awake at night," confessed Marina Benally, a dedicated teacher who has spent the past 7 years at the school.

Our work that day focused on addressing students' diverse needs in reading. This was an urgent problem of practice, and one that would not be easily undertaken without collective and focused effort. The school itself experienced nearly continuous change over the 6 years I had been working there as a consultant: High student turnover, erratic attendance, and high attrition after basketball season were accompanied by yearly changes in teaching staff and school leadership. The work of improving students' reading was not, therefore, merely a matter of implementing strategies or purchasing new curriculum. With only 29% of 10th-grade students passing the state test in reading in the 2010–2011 school year, the situation required intensive collaboration of teachers and principals to implement systemic changes that would be responsive to students' needs.

Teachers identified a list of students whose reading, engagement, and achievement in school were cause for concern. Working from this list, we set out to learn techniques for reading assessment and to practice with Heritage students. We hoped better assessment would reveal why students struggled in school, and how we could respond through classroom instruction. Our first student, Wilson (a pseudonym), bravely agreed to read for us while we took running records.[1] We then asked him to talk about his reading process and experience. By the time we finished the assessment, we had discovered that Wilson was reading at a 3rd-grade level and that he often felt as though when he read something, he quickly forgot it.

"That must be really frustrating," Marina said.

Wilson nodded. "When we do sticky notes in language arts class," he said, "it helps me to write down what I read so I can remember—otherwise I can't." Wilson also told us that he struggled most when the reading "isn't interesting to me," which explained much of the off-task behavior teachers were seeing from him in the classroom.

After Wilson left the room, we debriefed our observations and the implications for instruction. "How do we do this?" teachers wondered aloud. "I feel like I have to start teaching at an elementary school level. We put in so much time making the curriculum meaningful for our students, finding resources to help them understand their history and culture; what do we do now?"

GOING BEYOND THE CLASSROOM TEACHER: THE CASE FOR SOCIALLY JUST LEADERSHIP

It pains me to hear teachers ask these questions—not because they aren't the right questions, but because they should not have to face the solutions alone. The solutions require a coordinated, multifaceted response from the educational system in order to make the difference needed in the classroom. Assessments and interventions cannot occur without intense professional development, release time, and the active support and involvement of the school principal and district leadership to allot time and funding for teacher collaboration. The assessments cannot be useful without further opportunities for professional learning to determine how to restructure students' learning opportunities across the school day, provide varying levels of support (e.g., intensive individual and small-group reading support), and determine the exact focus and strategies needed for instructional intervention. None of this will do any good without the resources—assessments and appropriately leveled texts—needed to address what students need as readers.

All this requires instructional leaders who can advocate and organize for the conditions needed to support teachers and students in a systematic and sustained way. The problems teachers face in schools like Heritage cannot be addressed through any single strategy or approach—nor can they be solved in a month or even a single school year. But I truly believe they *can* be solved, and the solutions require focused collaborative leadership and learning at all levels of the educational system.

The work of middle and high school reform is complex because we must create conditions for adult and student learning—and learning takes time. Many struggling students attend struggling schools composed of staffs that do not yet know how to work collaboratively on problems of practice in teaching and learning. These schools are not well served by mandates and benchmarks unless they have the leadership and support needed for comprehensive change—in school culture, in the daily educational structures that affect learning, and in the instruction that takes place in the classroom. These changes require more than just cosmetic reorganization; they require us to fundamentally refocus and reorganize the daily life of schools to ensure learning at all levels: for teachers and school leaders, as well as for students.

Within district- and school-level educational systems, leadership for social justice can ideally come from the collaboration of teacher leaders and administrators. Such nonhierarchical collaboration is needed to foster the kinds of educational communities that can support and sustain visionary work in the classroom. Instructional leadership for social justice makes decisions that are accountable to two overarching questions:

1. How will a given decision or action best serve and support students' learning—especially for those students who are socially or academically marginalized?
   » How will the decision or action improve students' access to learning?
   » How will the decision or action create opportunities for students to acquire positive social identities and positions that support their academic achievement?
   » What stance (toward students, teachers, and learning) is reflected in this decision or action—and how does this model socially just pedagogy?
   » How will the decision or action facilitate students' agency with regard to their own learning?
2. How will a given decision best equip teachers—as learners and professionals—to meet students' needs through socially just instruction?

To be clear: Leadership for change requires that we make learning work central—and that we understand learning as a process that requires thoughtful planning and continuous care. In order for students to learn differently, teachers must teach adaptively. Teacher learning for continuous improvement requires leadership and site-based opportunities for studying classroom practice and planning based on instructional implications if we are to continually improve the craft of teaching.

In a recent article on the practices of school principals who work effectively for social justice, Theoharis (2011) outlined how those principals' actions created conditions for meaningful change that affected marginalized students' experiences and achievement in school. Among these were efforts to dismantle school structures such as tracking and pullout programs that segregate students and limit their access to rich and rigorous learning, as well as efforts to improve the professional capacity of staff through professional development opportunities. Effective principals, Theoharis found, actively supervised and worked with teachers to ensure that the school environment was inclusive and equitable for all students and that teachers had the necessary training and resources to do the job. These principals developed and capitalized on teacher leadership to empower staff—yet kept a tight rein on the vision and expectations for creating schools that could transform disparities in achievement, attendance, and engagement. In short, their role was critical for creating socially just school environments that could grow and flourish beyond the work of individual teachers in their classrooms.

Theoharis notes that while many school reform efforts have emphasized the role of professional development, what differed in the leadership practice of the principals he studied was how professional learning was tied to issues of equity and justice. In one elementary school, for example, the principal noted that English language learner (ELL) students were the most marginalized and underserved population. She therefore required all staff to receive training in how to work with ELL students, and enabled teachers to gain ELL certification to better equip them to serve their neediest students. In the next section, I outline several ways leadership practice can support the aims of socially just teaching and learning.

PUTTING SOCIALLY JUST LEADERSHIP INTO ACTION

Leadership for social justice means taking a stand to prioritize and focus on the needs of our most vulnerable students—not those of the adults in the learning system. This is a hard line to walk. I have known many a committed teacher who, in addition to pouring many hours of time into her practice, is required to expend a great deal of energy engaging with resistant (and at times hostile) colleagues who actively work to obstruct efforts aimed at improving equity and achievement for underserved students. The work we do as teachers is too urgent and too important for us to spend precious time engaged in adult conflicts that do nothing to serve the needs of students, yet I find time and again that this is often what consumes a great deal of valuable time.

Effective school leaders I have worked with know how to organize around teachers who make an effort to inquire into their own practice, who engage in reflective practice to understand the needs of students, and who can foster collaboration around the work of planning for instruction from careful study and assessment. When we put our energy where the hope is, and when teachers experience the power of collaborating for transformative purposes, we sow the seeds for changing school cultures and create conditions conducive to socially just teaching and learning.

To that end, I offer several points for consideration and action that can guide the work of school leaders. Drawing on the framework for socially just teaching practice, we can consider how leadership practice may be informed by many of the same principles.

The first principle: Develop a leadership stance of inquiry, collaboration, and continuous improvement toward specific goals for student learning. Effective principals I have known view themselves as lead learners and work to develop the culture needed to foster learning-oriented schools. They help to frame social justice problems of practice around students' learning needs and join teachers in shared study of those problems. As they take a stance of shared inquiry, their supervision of teachers focuses on observing classroom instruction, posing questions focused on shared areas of inquiry, and providing formative coaching (Nidus & Sadder, 2011) toward the goal of supporting classroom instruction that helps to address the needs of all, and particularly the most vulnerable, students. In assuming this stance, principals can partner with teachers to make sense of what students need for their learning and what teachers need for their practice.

This stance also affords school leaders a better position from which to have voice in the culture and direction of the school. Principals' presence in professional learning and in meaningful, grounded conversations about the challenges of classroom practice for socially just objectives communicates to teachers that "we are doing the work of addressing problems of practice together. I have expectations that we work together productively and effectively, and that we make progress, but I am here to provide support as well in order to help us all serve students better."

Unfortunately, not all teachers share the values and vision of socially just education. Improving school cultures and working to address inequities at the school and classroom level does not happen without conflict and resistance, some of which serves to protect vested interests in maintaining the status quo, even if it is at students' expense. Leadership for social justice requires that we not avoid the conflict that comes inevitably with a change process, but that we instead frame conflicts around the needs of students and the call to do what is right for our most vulnerable students rather than what is "equal" or convenient.

The second principle: Choose a focus that prioritizes the needs of the most vulnerable students. For any school leaders, including teacher leaders, who seek to create more just educational conditions in school, there are several key questions that might guide planning for professional learning to advance social justice objectives:

- What does my data say about which groups of students are most underserved and how can professional learning focus on meeting the needs of those students?
- What goals for student learning will focus and drive our efforts? What aspects of literacy instruction and learning will be prioritized?
- How will the supports and structures I create best enable teachers to learn, reflect, and act in ways that develop sustainable practices for socially just teaching and learning?

Although the problems facing many struggling schools can lead one to distraction by their sheer number alone, choosing a clear, manageable focus is essential for putting conditions in place that can support student and teacher growth. At Mount Rainier High School, for example, principal Julie Hunter and her leadership team named the following goal for their school community:"Staff will understand and use formative assessment to inquire into student learning and use it to inform practice." While many staff expressed frustration at trying to meet the needs of a diverse student population, Julie noticed that many teachers needed more tools and support for assessing how and why students struggled, and that time spent in department meetings often did not reflect a shared focus on making sense of students' needs as learners and how to address them through instruction. By naming the primary focus for adult learning and how it would support students' learning, Julie helped to restructure department meetings as professional learning communities focused on sharing student work and problems of practice. Her emphasis on helping teams focus on identifying students of concern brought more collective attention to ensuring that those students could be successful when teachers learned more about how to adapt their instruction and provide differentiation and support.

Whatever the goal for a given school context, it must be firmly tied to improving students' learning. This must drive other decisions that relate to the goal, such as how professional learning opportunities will be structured and how supervision and coaching will be focused. In order to grow and sustain conditions for socially just teaching and learning, teachers and students must feel that the goals and purposes are clear and relevant. Just as with good classroom instruction, good building leadership makes the objectives, purpose, and process for collective learning clear.

The third principle: Identify corresponding areas of instructional practice that offer the greatest potential for affecting students' access to learning, given the goal. Using assessment of students' needs to drive the learning work of schools ensures that the instructional strategies emphasized through professional development serve a clear purpose. Implementation of reading strategies or inquiry-based learning, no matter how well researched as good practices, do not serve a large enough purpose unless they play a clear and explicit role in helping students achieve better and more equitably.

In their review of initiatives aimed at improving students' access to powerful instruction in high schools, Corcoran and Silander (2009) identify several promising areas for professional learning that can serve to focus efforts to improve classroom instruction. They note specifically that the areas of inquiry-based learning, reading and writing across curriculum, and formative assessment show promise for elevating student achievement. Yet their conclusions offer a more complex view of the kind of work needed in high schools. While the areas named for instructional improvement provide a valuable focus, the authors argue that what is ultimately needed is to help teachers use pedagogical knowledge to engage in *adaptive instruction*, based on students' needs. While developing pedagogical expertise in particular areas of literacy learning certainly matters, instructional strategies are not ends unto themselves. These areas of focus hold the greatest promise for professional development when tied meaningfully to instructional processes for assessment, reflection, and supported implementation.

The fourth principle: Develop communities of practice based on assessment, observation, planning, and learning grounded in classroom work with real—and specific—students. To support teacher learning and practice in alignment with socially just goals, school leaders can create learning opportunities tied to classroom practice. My work with the Marysville School District, for example, focused on working with high school teachers to assess and develop units of study for student outcomes in reading and writing. Because many students struggle to read critically, for example, we developed a unit focused on how to read arguments in persuasive texts. Working with a core group of teacher leaders, sessions focused on demonstrating and trying out the reading work we wanted students to do, engaging in and co-planning sample lessons inside the unit, and trying out instruction in one classroom over time. Each time we worked in the classroom, teachers observed and collaboratively assessed students' learning in order to reflect on instructional approaches and adapt instruction based on students' needs. In follow-up meetings at the middle and end of unit implementation, teachers brought their own student work to share and worked collaboratively to calibrate assessment, identify areas for student growth, and support one another in planning for classroom interventions.

Once communities of practice have been created to support adaptive instruction, school leaders can help teacher communities develop action plans based on their work together and facilitate an ongoing focus on equity and social justice. Leaders can help groups focus their professional learning around work with their most challenging classes and with the students who struggle most. Marysville teachers, for example, chose five struggling students as case studies and focused on developing their assessment and gathering student work from those five. A case study approach can provide a depth of understanding about students' diverse needs and can create a manageable focus for study. I have found that when I teach any given class, I carry with me the lessons that different students have taught me about how they engage in literacy learning and how my instruction can support—or impede—their development as readers and writers. Professional learning opportunities need to help teachers make sense of the learning diversity they experience every day and the implications for their instruction.

Professional learning communities have been advocated as an important strategy in the work of school improvement (DuFour, Eaker, & DuFour, 2005). In practice, however, the work of developing strong communities of teachers can require active facilitation and oversight; simply putting people into groups doesn't ensure good learning or the kind of healthy collaboration that can lead to changes in student outcomes. Effective principals need to balance and differentiate support for staff so that teacher leaders have the conditions needed to remain at the vanguard of efforts to develop socially just practice while those who are resistant receive more structure for engagement.

The fifth principle: Help communities of practice develop understanding of the sociocultural nature of literacy learning and implications for students' reading and interactions in the classroom. Given the importance of texts and ideas to the goals of socially just pedagogy, it is vital that we develop both theoretical and practical understandings of the reading process as a means by which those goals might be achieved. Although recent developments in literacy education have supported the more explicit teaching of metacognition and strategies for comprehension and meaning making (Harvey & Goudvis, 2007; Keene & Zimmerman, 1997; Schoenbach et al., 1999), Hammerberg (2004) notes that approaches to the teaching of reading within many English language arts classrooms in the United States still lack many important aspects of sociocultural theories. She writes:

> With a socio-culturally relevant approach to comprehension instruction, texts and reading situations are always open for negotiation. The characters, plots, signs, and symbols of a text do not demand a singular interpretation, and they are not stuck to a singular meaning. Instead, they are open to many possible interpretations and meanings, and readers here are assumed to be interactive participants in creating meanings relevant for a particular situation. The many possible interpretations and meanings come from choosing how to react and interact with the text (which textual aspects to pay attention to, identify with, or explore further), and children (all children) are seen as capable of seeking these connections. (p. 654)

An explicit focus on comprehension strategies in the classroom cannot suffice as a means to address students' needs as readers. Professional learning opportunities should help teachers acquire sociocultural strategies for the teaching of reading so they can work more powerfully with their students. Classrooms that support diverse readers provide opportunities to consider multiple readings and perspectives and to critically analyze and respond to them, while maintaining the power and dignity of readers to make meanings in their own right. As Melissa, the teacher described in Chapters 5 and 6, noted, teachers need explicit knowledge and tools to effectively construct such classrooms and opportunities.

Leaders can support professional learning in this area. One way is to support teachers' study of the teaching of reading within a socially just framework, such as the one outlined in Chapter 1. As a means to create professional learning communities, study groups can include the close examination and analysis of classroom reading events (observed or videotaped) as part of the learning process. Teachers and leaders could analyze the reading events as a form of student work, using students' discourse and interactions during the event as grounds for the following inquiries:

1. What meanings are students making—individually and collectively— with a particular text?
2. Why might they be making those meanings in this context? In other words, how are students' meanings potentially shaped by the classroom context and how might they in turn shape that context and students' reading work?
3. What implications do particular meanings have for particular readers in this context?
4. How are students' identities positioned via the teacher, texts, activities, and meaning-making events?

Chapter 6 offers tools for analysis, reflection, and action that can inform such communities of practice.

Helping teachers to analyze students' reading with a sociocultural lens can also support their critical study of power in the classroom. Teachers can then use the process of reflecting on practice to understand students' needs for learning and to plan for adaptive instruction.

Building more socially just schools and classrooms is a tall order—for teachers and school leaders. Melissa noted to me on several occasions that although she had taken a course on social justice education as part of her master's degree and certification, the nature of the course was highly theoretical and the practical realities of implementation infinitely more complex. Melissa was deeply committed to the ideals of social justice and to teaching in ways that made a difference for her students, so she continually reflected on her practice to take on these challenges. Supportive communities of practice can go a long way toward nurturing socially just practice for teachers in schools where effective, transformative teaching is desperately needed.

CONCLUSION

As an educator committed to the goals of socially just pedagogy, I share teachers' frustrations at the difficulty of this work—and the enduring hope that socially just teaching can make a difference. Boyd et al. (2006) remind us that

> the first step toward creating equitable literacy classrooms—and to leave no student behind—is to acknowledge that English teachers and teacher educators are complicit in the reproduction of racial and socioeconomic inequality all across U.S. schools. . . . Teaching is a political act, and in our preparation of future teachers and citizens, teachers and teacher educators need to be advocates for and models of social justice and equity. (p. 331)

Teachers cannot enact socially just practice in isolation and should not be alone in their efforts to address inequities. In order for socially just pedagogy to become broadly and meaningfully applied, teachers and school leaders need to model socially just practices and processes and create school cultures built on these ways of working. Leaders can support teachers' ongoing learning, then, by considering how their own practices model socially just pedagogy within school contexts and in the kinds and quality of the learning opportunities and structures they provide for teachers to do the work.

However support is provided, it is vitally needed. Without it, committed teachers like Melissa, Ervanna, Marina, and Alissa can easily burn out when confronted by the challenges of socially just teaching in the complex worlds of schools and classrooms. Without it, educators who do not share their commitments may further perpetuate the very Discourses and practices that sustain persistent and institutionalized patterns of injustice.

Education plays a critical role in creating a more socially just society, one in which an individual's social class, race, ethnicity, gender, or sexual orientation should not serve as a means of exclusion or a socially constructed barrier to their aspirations. When students learn more, they are better empowered to use their literacy and knowledge to contribute productively as citizens. And when all students have access to a powerful and empowering education, we move closer to becoming the democracy of our ideals, built on principles of equity, justice, and opportunity. I have high hopes that the world of reading, learning, and social interaction in the socially just classroom constructs a vision of what is possible for a better society. This is most certainly hard work, but with shared vision and commitment, I believe it can be done.

Notes

Chapter 5

1. The school and city name, as well as the names of all research participants in this study, are pseudonyms. Students in the class chose their own pseudonyms. Data collected for research included video and field notes taken during class, as well as in- and out-of-school interviews with 8 case study readers (out of a class of 20). Case study readers consisted of 2 White males, 2 African American males, 3 African American females, and 1 White female.

The research used constant comparative (Glaser & Strauss, 1967; Strauss & Corbin, 1990) and critical discourse analytic (Gee, 1996; Fairclough, 1995) methods to study students' processes of reading and meaning making with texts in the English language arts classroom and how they brought their racial and ethnic subjectivity and identity to bear on that process.

2. Throughout the chapter, the speaker's self-described racial identity is noted to show how classroom and conversational dynamics were shaped by race. Self-described White students are designated using (W) and self-described African American students are designated using (AA). Several students chose to identify themselves as Black, and their names are therefore accompanied by (B).

Chapter 6

1. I use the symbol ~ here to indicate the gist, rather than the exact wording, of Jade's comment. While I noted her comment during class discussion in my field notes, then listened to the videotape to get her exact wording as much as possible, she is a very soft-spoken student and it was difficult to make out each word. She made this same point more than once, however, so my paraphrase reflects the content of her idea.

Chapter 8

1. Running records are a means of oral reading assessment developed by Marie Clay (1993).

References

Alexie, S. (2007). *The absolutely true diary of a part-time Indian*. Boston: Little, Brown.

Alliance for Excellent Education. (2009). *High school dropouts in America*. Retrieved from the Alliance for Excellent Education website: http://www.all4ed.org/publication_material/GradDropout_Rates

Allington, R. (2007). Effective teachers, effective instruction. In K. P. Beers (Ed.), *Adolescent literacy: Turning promise into practice* (pp. 273–288). Portsmouth, NH: Heinemann.

Alper, D. (Producer), & Muccino, G. (Director). (2006). *The pursuit of happyness* (motion picture). United States: Columbia Pictures.

Alvermann, D. (2002). Effective literacy instruction for adolescents. *Journal of Literacy Research, 34*(2), 189–208.

Anderson, R. C., & Pearson, P. D. (1984). A schema-theoretic view of basic processes in reading. In P. D. Pearson (Ed.), *Handbook of reading research* (pp. 255–291). New York: Longman.

Atwell, N. (1998). *In the middle: New understandings about writing, reading, and learning*. Portsmouth, NH: Heinemann.

Austen, J. (1992). *Mansfield Park*. Hertfordshire, UK: Wordsworth Editions Limited. (Original work published 1814).

Banning, M. (1999). Race, class, gender, and classroom discourse. In L. Parker, D. Deyhle, & S. Villenas (Eds.), *Race is . . . race isn't: Critical race theory and qualitative studies in education* (pp. 155–180). Boulder, CO: Westview Press.

Ballenger, C. (1999). *Teaching other people's children: Literacy and learning in a bilingual classroom*. New York: Teachers College Press.

Banks, J. (2001). *Cultural diversity and education: Foundations, curriculum, and teaching*. Boston: Allyn & Bacon.

Beah, I. (2007). *A long way gone: Memoirs of a boy soldier*. New York: Farrar, Strauss, and Giroux.

Beers, K., Probst, R., & Rief, L. (2007). *Adolescent literacy: Turning promise into practice*. Portsmouth, NH: Heinemann.

Beloni, L. F., & Jongsma, E. A. (1978). The effects of interest on reading comprehension of low-achieving students. *Journal of Reading, 22*(2), 106–109.

Blau, S. (2003). Performative literacy: The habits of mind of highly literate readers. *Voices from the Middle, 10*(3), 18–22.

Bomer, R. (1995). *Time for meaning*. Portsmouth, NH: Heinemann.

Bomer, R., &. Bomer, K. (2001). *For a better world: Reading and writing for social action*. Portsmouth, NH: Heinemann.

Bourne, J., & Jewitt, C. (2004, April). *"Two blushing pilgrims" and "the Haj thing": The impact of cultural and linguistic diversity on reader positioning in urban secondary English classrooms.* Paper presented at the American Educational Research Association Conference, San Diego, CA.

Boyd, F., Ariail, M., Williams, R., Jocson, K., Sachs, G. T., McNeal, K. . . . , & Morrell, E. (2006). Real teaching for real diversity: Preparing English Language Arts teachers for 21st-century classrooms. *English Education Special Issue: A Report on the CEE Summit. 38*(4), 329–350.

Boykin, A. W., & Noguera, P. (2011). *Creating the opportunity to learn: Moving from research to practice to close the achievement gap.* Alexandria, VA: ASCD.

Bransford, J. D., Brown, A. L., & Cocking, R. R. (Eds.). (2000). *How people learn: Brain, mind, and school.* Washington, DC: National Academy Press.

Cambourne, B. (1995). Toward an educationally relevant theory of literacy learning: Twenty years of inquiry. *The Reading Teacher, 49*(3), 182–187.

Christensen, L. (2000). *Reading, writing, and rising up: Teaching about social justice and the power of the written word.* Milwaukee, WI: Rethinking Schools (www.rethinkingschools.org).

Cisneros, S. (1991). *The house on Mango Street.* New York: Vintage.

City, E., Elmore, R., Fiarman, S., & Teitel, L. (2009). *Instructional rounds in education: A network approach to improving teaching and learning.* Cambridge, MA: Harvard Education Press.

Clay, M. (1993). *An observation of early literacy achievement.* Portsmouth, NH: Heinemann.

Corcoran, T., & Silander, M. (2009). Instruction in high schools: The evidence and the challenge. *Teachers College Record, 19*(1), 157–183.

Cummins, J. (2007). Pedagogies for the poor? Realigning reading instruction for low-income students with scientifically based reading research. *Educational Researcher, 36*(9), 564–572.

Darling-Hammond, L., & Richardson, N. (2009). Teaching learning: What matters? *Educational Leadership, 66*(5), 46–55.

Delpit, L., & Dowdy, J. K. (Eds.). (2002). *The skin that we speak: Thoughts on language and culture in the classroom.* New York: The New Press.

DuFour, R., Eaker, R., & DuFour, R. (Eds.). (2005). *On common ground: The power of professional learning communities.* Bloomington, IN: SolutionTree.

Eggers, D. (2006). *What is the what.* New York: Vintage.

Elbow, P. (1986). *Embracing contraries: Explorations in learning and teaching.* New York: Oxford University Press.

Fairclough, N. (1995). *Critical discourse analysis.* Essex, UK: Pearson Education.

Fine, M., Weis, L., Powell, L. C., & Wong, L. M. (Eds.). (1997). *Off white: Readings in race, power, and society.* New York: Routledge.

Forsyth, D. R., & McMillan, J. H. (1981). Attributions, affect, and expectations: A test of Weiner's three-dimensional model. *Journal of Educational Psychology, 73*(3), 393–403.

Freire, P. (1972). *Pedagogy of the oppressed.* Harmondsworth, UK: Penguin.

Freire, P. (1994). *Pedagogy of hope: Reliving pedagogy of the oppressed.* (R. Barr, Trans.). New York: Continuum Press.

Gay, G. (2002). Preparing for culturally responsive teaching. *Journal of Teacher Education, 53*(2), 106–116.

Gee, J. P. (1996). *Social linguistics and literacies: Ideology in discourses* (2nd ed.). London: Falmer.

Gee, J. P. (1999). *An introduction to discourse analysis: Theory and method.* New York: Routledge.

Gee, J. P. (2001). Reading as situated language: A socio-cognitive perspective. *Journal of Adolescent and Adult Literacy, 44*(8): 714–725.

Glaser, B., & Strauss, A. (1967). *The discovery of grounded theory: Strategies for qualitative research.* New York: Aldin.

Golding, W. (1954). *Lord of the flies.* Boston: Faber and Faber.

Graham, S. (1994). Motivation in African Americans. *Review of Educational Research, 64*(1), 55–117.

Greene, S. (Ed.). (2008). *Literacy as a civil right: Reclaiming social justice in literacy teaching and learning.* New York: Peter Lang.

Guthrie, J. (2004). Teaching for literacy engagement. *Journal of Literacy Research, 36,* 1–30.

Hammerberg, D. (2004). Comprehension instruction for socioculturally diverse classrooms: A review of what we know. *Reading Teacher, 57*(7), 648–658.

Hansberry, L. (1988). *A raisin in the sun.* New York: Random House. (Original work published 1958).

Harris, C. I. (1995). Whiteness as property. In K. Crenshaw, N. Gotanda, G. Peller, & K. Thomas (Eds.), *Critical race theory: The key writings that formed the movement* (pp. 276–291). New York: The New Press.

Holschuh, J., Nist, S., & Olejnik, S. (2001). Attributions to failure: The effects of effort, ability, and learning strategy use on perceptions of future goals and emotional responses. *Reading Psychology, 22,* 1153–1173.

Hughes, L. (1994). Dreams. In *The collected poems of Langston Hughes* (p. 32). New York: Alfred A. Knopf/Vintage.

Hurston, Z. N. (1937). *Their eyes were watching God.* Philadelphia: Lippincott.

Ibsen, H. (2005). *A doll's house.* Clayton, DE: Prestwick House. (Original work published 1879).

Keene, E. O., & Zimmerman, S. (1997). *Mosaic of thought.* Portsmouth, NH: Heinemann.

Kress, R. (1989). Trends in remedial instruction. *Journal of Reading, 32*(4), 370–72.

Ladson-Billings, G. (2004). What is critical race theory and what is it doing in a nice field like education? In G. Ladson-Billings & D. Gillborn (Eds.), *The Routledge-Falmer reader in multicultural education* (pp. 49–67). New York: RoutledgeFalmer.

Ladson-Billings, G. (2000). Reading between the lines and beyond the pages: A culturally relevant approach to literacy teaching. In A. G. Hollingsworth (Ed.), *What counts as literacy: Challenging the school standard* (pp. 139–152). New York: Teachers College Press.

Lankshear, C., & McLaren, P. (1993). Critical literacy and the postmodern turn. In C. Lankshear & P. McLaren (Eds.), *Critical literacy: Politics, praxis, and the postmodern* (pp. 379–419). Albany: State University of New York Press.

Leander, K. (2002). Locating Latanya: The situated production of identity artifacts in classroom interaction. *Research in the Teaching of English, 37,* 198–250.

Lee, V. (2001). *Restructuring high schools for equity and excellence: What works*. New York: Teachers College Press.

Leonardo, Z. (2004). The souls of White folk: Critical pedagogy, Whiteness studies, and globalization discourse. In G. Ladson-Billings & D. Gillborn (Eds.), *The Routledge-Falmer reader in multicultural education* (pp. 116–136). New York: RoutledgeFalmer.

Lesko, N. (2001). *Act your age! A cultural construction of adolescence*. New York: RoutledgeFalmer.

Lotan, R. (2006). Teaching teachers to build equitable classrooms. *Theory into Practice, 45*(1), 32–39.

Maher, F., & Tetreault, M. K. (1997). Learning in the dark: How assumptions of Whiteness shape classroom knowledge. *Harvard Educational Review, 67*(2), 321–349.

McCormick, P. (2006). *Sold*. New York: Hyperion.

Mellor, B., & Patterson, A. (2000). Critical practice: Teaching "Shakespeare." *Journal of Adolescent and Adult Literacy, 43*(6), 508–517.

Mercer, N. (2002). Developing dialogues. In G. Wells & G. Claxton (Eds.), *Learning for life in the 21st Century: Sociocultural perspectives on the future of education*. (pp. 141–153). Oxford, UK: Blackwell.

Mercer, N., Wegerif, R., & Dawes, L. (1999). Children's talk and the development of reasoning in the classroom. *British Education Research Journal, 25*(1), 95–111.

Miller, S. (1986). *The good mother*. New York: Dell.

Mishima, Y. (1994). *The sound of waves*. (M. Weatherby, Trans.). New York: Vintage. (Original work published 1954).

Moje, E. B., Dillon, D. R., & O'Brien, D. (2000). Reexamining roles of learner, text, and context in secondary literacy. *The Journal of Educational Research, 93*(3): 165–180.

Moll, L. C. (1992). Bilingual classroom studies and community analysis. *Educational Researcher, 21*(8), 5–14.

Morrison, T. (1987). *Beloved*. New York: Penguin.

Myers, W. D. (1999). *Monster*. New York: HarperCollins.

Ng, R. (Ed.). (1995). *Anti-racism, feminism, and critical approaches to education*. Westport, CT: Greenwood.

Nidus, G., & Sadder, M. (2011). The principal as formative coach. *Educational Leadership, 69*(2), 30–35.

Noguera, P. (2007). *School reform and second-generation discrimination: Toward the development of equitable schools*. Providence, RI: Annenberg Institute for School Reform.

North, C. E. (2006). More than words? Delving into the substantive meaning(s) of "social justice" in education. *Review of Educational Research. 76*(4), 507–535.

North, C. E. (2009). *Teaching for social justice? Voices from the front lines*. Boulder, CO: Paradigm.

Nystrand, M. (1997). *Opening dialogue: Understanding the dynamics of language and learning in the English classroom*. New York: Teachers College Press.

Nystrand, M. (2006). Research on the role of classroom discourse as it affects reading comprehension. *Research in the Teaching of English, 40*(4), 392–412.

Nystrand, M., & Gamoran, A. (1991). Instructional discourse, student engagement, and literate achievement. *Research in the Teaching of English, 25*, 261–290.

O'Connor, C. (1997). Dispositions toward (collective) struggle and educational resilience in the inner city: A case analysis of six African-American high school students. *American Educational Research Journal, 34*(4), 593–629.

Ogbu, J. (2003). *Black American students in an affluent suburb: A study of academic disengagement.* Mahwah, NJ: Lawrence Erlbaum Associates.

Ong, W. (2002). The writer's audience is always a fiction. In T. J. Farrell & P. A. Soukup (Eds.), *The Ong reader: Challenges for further inquiry.* Cresskill, NJ: Hampton Press.

Oyserman, D., Gant, L., & Ager, J. (1995). A socially contextualized model of African American identity: Possible selves and school persistence. *Journal of Personality and Social Psychology, 69*(6), 1216–1232.

Paley, V. (1979). *White teacher.* Cambridge, MA: Harvard University Press.

Paulsen, G. (1993). *Nightjohn.* New York: Bantam Doubleday Dell.

Pearson, P. D., & Gallagher, M. (1983). *The instruction of reading comprehension.* Champaign: University of Illinois, Center for the Study of Reading.

Pixley, M., & VanDerPloeg, L. S. (2000). Learning to see: White. *English Education, 32*(4), 278–279.

Plaut, S. (Ed.). (2009). *The right to literacy in secondary schools: Creating a culture of thinking.* New York: Teachers College Press.

Resnick, L. (1999). From aptitude to effort: A new foundation for our schools. *American Educator, 23*(1), 14–17.

Rex, L. (2000). Judy constructs a genuine question: A case for interactional inclusion. *Teaching and Teacher Education, 16*(2000), 315–333.

Rex, L. (2001). The remaking of a high school reader. *Reading Research Quarterly, 36*(3), 288–314.

Rex, L., & Schiller, L. (2009). *Using discourse analysis to improve classroom interaction.* New York: Routledge.

Ritchhart, R. (2002). *Intellectual character: What it is, why it matters, and how to get it.* San Francisco: Jossey-Bass.

Rogers, R. (2002). Between contexts: A critical discourse analysis of family literacy, discursive practices, and literate subjectivities. *Reading Research Quarterly, 37*(3), 248–277.

Rosenblatt, L. (1993). The transactional theory: Against dualisms. *College English, 55*(4), 377–386.

Rosenblatt, L. (2004). The transactional theory of reading and writing. In R. B. Ruddell & N. J. Unrau (Eds.), *Theoretical models and processes of reading* (5th ed., pp. 1363–1398). Newark, DE: International Reading Association.

Ruddell, R. B., & Speaker, R., Jr. (1985). The interactive reading process: A model. In R. B. Ruddell & H. Singer (Eds.), *Theoretical models and processes of reading* (pp. 751–793). Newark, DE: International Reading Association.

Rumelhart, D. E. (1994). Toward an interactive model of reading. In R. B. Ruddell, M. R. Ruddell, & H. Singer (Eds.), *Theoretical models and processes of reading* (4th ed., pp. 864–894). Newark, DE: International Reading Association.

Ryckman, D. B., & Peckham, P. (1987). Gender differences in attributions for success and failure situations across subject areas. *Journal of Educational Research, 81*(2), 120–125.

Sanders, W. L., & Horn, S. P. (1998). Research findings from the Tennessee value-added system (TVAAS) database: Implications for educational evaluation and research. *Journal of Personnel Evaluation in Education, 12*(3), 247–256.

Santa Barbara Discourse Group. (1994). Constructing literacy in classrooms: Literate action as social accomplishment. In R. B. Ruddell, M. R. Ruddell, & H. Singer (Eds.), *Theoretical models and processes of reading* (4th ed., pp. 124–154). Newark, DE: International Reading Association.

Schoenbach, R., Greenleaf, C., Cziko, C., & Hurwitz, L. (1999). *Reading for understanding: A guide to improving reading in middle and high school classrooms*. San Francisco: Jossey-Bass.

Shnayer, S. W., & Robinson, L. A. (1969). An analysis of phonic systems for the primary grades in eight basal reader series. *Reading Specialist, 9*(2), 58–72.

Shor, I., & Freire, P. (1985). *A pedagogy for liberation: Dialogues on transforming education*. Westport, CT: Bergin & Garvey.

Shor, I., & Freire, P. (1987). What is the "dialogical method" of teaching? *Journal of Education, 169*(3), 11–13.

Sizer, T. (1984). *Horace's compromise*. Boston: Houghton Mifflin.

Sleeter, C. E. (2004). How White teachers construct race. In G. Ladson-Billings & D. Gillborn (Eds.), *The Routledge Falmer reader in multicultural education* (pp. 163–178). New York: RoutledgeFalmer.

Sleeter, C. E., & Bernal, D. (2004). Critical pedagogy, critical race theory, and antiracist education: Implications for multicultural education. In J. A. Banks & C. A. McGee Banks (Eds.), *Handbook of research on multicultural education* (2nd ed.). San Francisco: Jossey-Bass.

Sperling, M. (2003). Tenth-grade literacy and the mediation of culture, race, and class. In S. Greene & D. Abt-Perkins (Eds.), *Making race visible: Literacy research for cultural understanding* (pp. 131–148). New York: Teachers College Press.

Steele, C. (1997). A threat in the air. *American Psychologist, 52*, 623–629.

Strauss, A. L., & Corbin, J. (1990). *Basics of qualitative research: Grounded theory procedures and techniques*. Newbury Park, CA: Sage.

Theoharis, G. (2011). Principals narrate the strategies they use to improve their schools and advance social justice. *Teachers College Record, 112*(1), 331–373. Retrieved from http://tcrecord.org. ID Number: 15842

Tolstoy, L. (2001). *Anna Karenina* (R. P. Volokhonsky & L. Volokhonsky, Trans.). New York: Penguin. (Original work published 1877).

Van den Branden, K. (2000). Does negotiation of meaning promote reading comprehension? A study of multilingual primary school classes. *Reading Research Quarterly, 35*, 426–443.

Weiner, B. (1985). An attributional theory of achievement motivation and emotion. *Psychological Review, 92*(4), 548–573.

Wood, D. J., Bruner, S., & Ross, G. (1976). The role of tutoring in problem solving. *Journal of Child Psychiatry and Child Psychology, 17*, 89–100.

Yun, J. T., & Moreno, J. F. (2006). College access, K–12 concentrated disadvantage, and the next 25 years of education research. *Educational Researcher, 35*(1), 12–19.

Index

A page number followed by a *t, f,* or *n* denotes a table, figure, or endnote, respectively.